# STRUGGLES FOR
# SOLIDARITY

# STRUGGLES FOR SOLIDARITY

## Liberation Theologies in Tension

Lorine M. Getz and
Ruy O. Costa
EDITORS

FORTRESS PRESS   Minneapolis

STRUGGLES FOR SOLIDARITY
Liberation Theologies in Tension

Scripture quotations unless otherwise noted are from the Revised Standard Version of the Bible, copyright © 1946, 1952, and 1971 by the Division of Christian Education of the National Council of Churches.

Excerpts from "Canon of Puerto Rican Nostalgia" from *Prophets Denied Honor: An Anthology of the Hispanic Church in the United States,* ed. Antonio M. Stevens-Arroyo, copyright © 1980 Orbis Books. Reprinted by permission.

Excerpts from "Cloud of Smoke, Pillar of Fire," by Irving Greenberg from *Auschwitz: Beginning of a New Era?* ed. Eva Fleischner, copyright © 1977 KTAV Publishing House, Inc. Reprinted by permission.

Excerpts from *The Jew as Pariah: Jewish Identity and Politics in the Modern Age* by Hannah Arendt, ed. Ron H. Feldman (New York: Grove Press, Inc., 1978). Reprinted by permission.

Excerpts from *Their Eyes Were Watching God* by Zora Neale Hurston, copyright © 1937 by Harper & Row, Publishers, Inc. Copyright renewed 1965 by John C. Hurston and Joel Hurston. Reprinted by permission of HarperCollins, Publishers, Inc.

Excerpts from *The House of the Spirits* by Isabel Allende, trans. M. Bogin. Translation copyright © 1985 by Alfred A. Knopf, Inc. Reprinted by permission of the publisher.

"Stop Your Singing!" from *Poesias* by Fernando Pessoa (Lisbon: Atica, SA Editores e Livreiros, 1978). Reprinted by permission.

Cover design by Carol Evans-Smith

Interior design by The Book Company/Wendy Calmenson

Library of Congress Cataloging-in-Publication Data

Struggles for solidarity : liberation theologies in tension /
    Lorine M. Getz and Ruy O. Costa, editors.
        p.    cm.
    Includes bibliographical references.
    ISBN 0-8006-2528-5
    1. Liberation theology.    2. Theology—20th century.
I. Getz, Lorine M.    II. Costa, Ruy O.
BT83.57.S78    1992
230'.046—dc20                                          91-33691
                                                       CIP

The paper used in this publication meets the minimum requirements of American National Standard for Information Sciences—Permanence of Paper for Printed Library Materials, ANSI Z329.48-1984.                                    ∞ ™

Manufactured in the U.S.A.                              AF 1-2528
96    95    94    93    92    1    2    3    4    5    6    7    8    9    10

*to the memory of*
*Orlando Costas*
*—friend and colleague—*

# Contents

## PART ONE

### STRUGGLE AND SOLIDARITY

7

# PART TWO

## DISCIPLINES IN DIALOGUE

# Preface

This book explores those thorny questions usually left unvoiced in discussions of liberation theology, problems that throw the various theologies of liberation into conflict with one another.

Focusing on the Americas, on key movements toward liberation of the whole American peoples, and on the perspectives of noted theological revisionists from the Christian and Jewish traditions, we hope through this work and the discourse that ensues to understand more clearly those obstacles to dialogue among various liberation theories and the culture-bound experiences of oppression from which they proceed. Out of these new insights, we hope, as theologians committed to human liberation, to move together beyond our differences and confusions toward solidarity.

In initiating a dialogue about obstacles to dialogue, we have faced a considerable editorial task. We have sought to center on the cutting edge issues and to entice articulate liberationists from the key Jewish and Christian schools and traditions on the American continents into our conversation. We invited them to participate in an exchange of seemingly conflictual or competing theories and experiences of oppression. Our aim has been to limit and shape this publication in ways that do justice to the passion, the commitments, and, at times, even the diametrically opposing views of our authors.

We extend special thanks to Lois Ruth Diesing, V. Mitchell Hay, David F. Kelly, Glenn Kohrmann, Richard T. Lauer, Brian McGrath, Carolyn Nikkal, and Diana S. Snow, who cheerfully assisted in the early stages of the book's production. To Michael West, Lois Torvik, and Philip Harden, we owe a debt of gratitude in adding the final touches to this lengthy editorial task.

Lorine M. Getz
Ruy O. Costa

# Contributors

*Rubem A. Alves*
Professor of philosophy at the Teacher's College of the State University of Campinas, Brazilian poet, psychoanalyst, and theologian, Rubem A. Alves is author of *A Theology of Human Hope* (Corpus Books, 1969), *Tomorrow's Child* (Harper & Row, 1972), *Protestantism and Repression: A Brazilian Case Study* (Orbis Books, 1985), *What Is Religion?* (Orbis Books, 1985), *I Believe in the Resurrection of the Body* (Fortress Press, 1986), and *The Poet, the Warrior, the Prophet* (TPI, 1990).

*James H. Cone*
Charles A. Briggs Distinguished Professor of Systematic Theology at Union Theological Seminary, New York City, James H. Cone is author of numerous articles and books, including *Black Theology and Black Power* (Harper & Row, 1969), *God of the Oppressed* (Harper & Row, 1978), *Black Theology: A Documentary History* (with Gayraud Wilmore, Orbis Books, 1979), *The Spirituals and the Blues: An Interpretation* (Harper & Row, 1980), *For My People: Black Theology and the Black Church* (Orbis Books, 1984), and *Martin and Malcolm and America: A Dream or a Nightmare* (Orbis Books, 1990).

*Ruy O. Costa*
Associate Director for Public Policy for the Massachusetts Council of Churches, Ruy O. Costa is the editor of *One Faith, Many Cultures* (BTI and Orbis Books, 1988).

11

*Orlando E. Costas*
Academic Dean and Judson Professor of Missiology at Andover Newton School of Theology until his death in 1987, Orlando E. Costas wrote *The Integrity of Mission: The Inner Life and Outreach of the Church* (Harper & Row, 1979), and *Liberating News: A Theology of Contextual Evangelization* (Eerdmans, 1989).

*Harvey G. Cox*
Victor S. Thomas Professor of Divinity at Harvard Divinity School, Harvey G. Cox is author of several books, including *The Secular City* (1965), *Religion in the Secular City* (Simon & Schuster, Inc., 1984), *The Silencing of Leonardo Boff: Liberation Theology and the Future of World Christianity* (Meyer Stone Books, 1988), and *Many Mansions: A Christian's Encounters with Other Faiths* (Beacon Press, 1988).

*Marc H. Ellis*
Professor of Religion, Culture, and Society Studies at the Maryknoll School of Theology, Marc H. Ellis is author of five books, including *Toward a Jewish Theology of Liberation: The Uprising and the Future* (Orbis Books, 1989), and *Beyond Innocence and Redemption: Confronting the Holocaust and Israeli Power* (Harper SF, 1990).

*Lorine M. Getz*
Associate Professor of Religious Studies and Coordinator of the Women's Studies Program at the University of North Carolina—Charlotte, Lorine M. Getz is author of *Nature and Grace in Flannery O'Connor's Fiction* (E. Mellen, 1982).

*Otto Maduro*
Venezuelan lay Catholic philosopher and sociologist of religion Otto Maduro, after four years of lecturing in the U.S.A., is presently writing his fifth book in Brazil—sponsored by the ISER (Rio de Janeiro) and the CESEP (São Paulo). Otto is both an advocate and a student of Latin American Liberation Theology, and recently finished editing *Judaism, Christianity, and Liberation: An Agenda for Dialogue* (Orbis Books, 1991).

*José Míguez Bonino*
Minister of the Argentine Evangelical Methodist Church, Professor Emeritus of Systematic Theology and Ethics of the Instituto Superior Evangelico de Estudios Teologicos in Buenos Aires, Argentina, José

Míguez Bonino is author of *Doing Theology in a Revolutionary Situation* (Fortress Press, 1975), *Toward a Christian Political Ethics* (Fortress Press, 1983), and editor of *Faces of Jesus: Latin American Christologies* (Orbis Books, 1984).

*Peter J. Paris*
Elmer G. Homrighausen Professor of Christian Social Ethics at Princeton Theological Seminary and President of the Society of Christian Ethics, Peter J. Paris is author of *The Social Teaching of the Black Churches* (Fortress Press, 1985), and *Black Religious Leaders: Conflict in Unity* (Westminster Press, 1991).

*Rosemary Radford Ruether*
Georgia Harkness Professor of Applied Theology at Garrett-Evangelical Theological Seminary, Rosemary Radford Ruether is author of many books, including *Sexism and God-Talk: Toward a Feminist Theology* (Beacon Press, 1984), *Women-Church: Theology and Practice* (Harper & Row, 1988), and *Disputed Questions: On Being a Christian* (Orbis Books, 1989).

*Pablo Richard*
Titular Professor of Theology at the National University and a member of DEI (Ecumenical Department of Research), Pablo Richard lives in Costa Rica and trains pastoral workers for Ecclesial Base Communities in Central America. His most recent works are: *The Idols of Death and the God of Life: A Theology* (Orbis Books, 1983), *Morte das Cristiandades e Nascimento de La Iglesia (Death of Christendoms, Birth of the Church,* Orbis Books, 1987), and *Naming the Idols: Biblical Alteratives for U.S. Foreign Policy* (Meyer Stone Books, 1988).

*Richard Shaull*
Henry Winters Luce Professor of Ecumenics Emeritus, Princeton Theological Seminary, Richard Shaull is author of *Heralds of a New Reformation: The Poor of South and North America* (Orbis Books, 1984) and *The Reformation and Liberation Theology* (Westminster/John Knox, 1991).

# Introduction

## Ruy O. Costa

As theologies of liberation encounter each other they refuse to reduce the other to an epiphenomenon of itself or to be reduced by the other as such. This is their dilemma: they need to talk in a way consistent with their irreducible mutual challenges as well as with their common agenda. Liberation theologies have moved quickly from monological discourses by oppressed communities in their particular struggles to a pluralism of discourses in debate over the nature of oppression and liberation to a search for a paradigm able to foster the naming of each particular oppression without fragmenting the oppressed communities into self-destructive warring factions. This is the subject of this book: liberation theologies' struggle for solidarity.

In a book on philosophy of education, Rubem Alves illustrates the struggle between dominated and dominant communities with a collection of delightful stories for children. In one of them, a certain "king Lion" determined that none of his subjects ought to die in ignorance, and so he drafted a team of buzzards, properly dressed in black doctoral robes, for the supervision of an educational project. Their first problem was to decide the curriculum, that is, to define what teachers should teach and students should learn. The team decided that

> the thoughts of the buzzards were the most true; the walking of the buzzards was the most elegant; the preferences of the buzzards' noses and palates were the best for a perfect health; the buzzards' color was the most tranquilizing; the singing of the buzzards was the most beautiful. (Alves 1984, 11)

15

Classes began. The teachers were very competent. Everybody understood everything quite clearly. Yet the students had alternative memories. The inner codes of their bodies knew nothing of the buzzards' reasons:

> After a class on the good smell and flavor of carrion one could see small groups of birds throwing up behind the trees, discreetly (in order not to offend their respectable teachers). . . . And the peacock and the parrots would not stop whispering: "Black is the most beautiful color? Bull. . . ." (Alves, 11)

The moral of the story is that "sometimes, the best evidence of intelligence is the refusal to learn." Alves calls this story "Pinocchio in Reverse." To him Pinocchio's story represents the best in psychoanalytic trickery:

> After leading a child to identify herself with a wooden doll the plot develops proclaiming that it is necessary to go to school in order to become human. Otherwise one's inevitable destiny is to become an ass, with tail, large ears, heehaws and everything else which belongs to asshood. Obviously this is a dishonest trick. It would be necessary to tell clearly what has been left untold here: the inverse destiny of those who were flesh and bones when they entered school and only got their diplomas after becoming wooden dolls. (Alves, 11)

Alves goes on to criticize the technocratic philosophy of education of the Brazilian school systems, which reduces Brazilian parrots and peacocks to functionaries of buzzard interests.

The buzzards' philosophy of education points to the monological worldview that has dominated much of Western philosophy until quite recently. A monological worldview presumes that there is only one correct way to interpret human life and experience in the world. Monological worldviews function as religious languages, from totemism to scientism. Emile Durkheim pointed to this aspect of religious experience when he defined the circle of the sacred as that which holds a whole cultural system together. He argued that logic is a social product. Religion is an elementary type of logic. Science is a more developed type of logic. Both share their social origin. Both function to hold a worldview together. That worldview is a tool conceived by the group for its own survival and development (Durkheim [1915] 1965). In the modern world the gods and totems of yesterday were replaced by science and technology. Herbert Marcuse's criticism of technologism is precisely that, in the modern world, the logic of efficiency has reduced the human experience (of the aesthetic, of the ludic [playful, pure pleasure], and so on) to functions of itself (Marcuse 1968).

In politics the monological spirit finds expression in doctrines that reduce the whole political process to one particular paradigm (for example, class conflict) and reduce all other struggles (for example, racism, sexism, and so on) to epiphenomena of that privileged paradigm. Both advanced capitalism and orthodox Marxism are monological; both are driven by the same logic of conquest and domination; each wants to convert the other into itself.

Monological languages cannot dialogue. They are self-enclosed, self-consistent, and self-sufficient systems. The moment a monological language opens up to dialogue, it renounces its internal monism and becomes dialogical. That is why any monological system has to define all competing systems as either illogical or as epiphenomena of itself. In interreligious relations, monologism takes the form of either holy wars or naive inclusivism of the syncretist type. In the latter, a dominant tradition declares its competitors to be part of its own tradition—emptying, therefore, the rationale for confrontation.

## THE ADVENT OF SOLIDARITY

Both holy wars and assimilation are antithetical to solidarity, for solidarity presumes mutually affirming, autonomous others. Solidarity is not the assimilation of the self into the other. Such assimilation is, in fact, a perversion of otherness, since otherness presumes differentiation. The absorption of the self into the other is an expression of love for the same. Enrique Dussel has formulated a concept of otherness from the perspective of those who have been denied status as "others" by the Western intellectual tradition, that is, Native Americans, women, children, and all the subjected others who are defined by the dominant world as functions of its totality. Dussel calls his method "anadialectical" in distinction from the various monistic dialects of domination of the tradition retrieved (Dussel 1977). The love of the same, however, is not the same as the love of self. The love of self is, in fact, the antithesis of the love of the same because it claims for the self its identity as an autonomous other in relation to the totality that wants to reduce it to an epiphenomenon of its own sameness. The love of the same is that passion for the construction of a world in one's own image and likeness—

like the buzzards' philosophy of education, like males' definition of the divine as male, like capitalism's unquenchable thirst for expansion.

Solidarity, as a community of mutually affirming, autonomous selves, is a project antithetical to the monological premises of the dominating status quo. One of the major dilemmas faced by the marginalized communities is precisely how to protect their particular identities without playing the self-destructive game of competition that the rules of the dominant status quo demand, that is, the game that sets one oppressed group against the other—the old Machiavellian divide-and-conquer game.

Competition is only one possible model of social interaction (Mannheim 1953, 74–164). It is, however, the model that obviously favors the player with the most resources—whether the game is tennis, boxing, or Wall Street. No wonder, then, that the players who have greater access to resources of power—wealth, organization, access to the media, and so on—insist on preaching the virtues of competition to those who have no choice, beside cooperation, but to denigrate themselves in the circus of the market. In direct competition against the big player, the little player is most likely to lose. When little players compete against each other (for jobs, as an example), the big one also wins (as with the lowering of wages to be paid). Besides, competition to excel in a game not one's own will only lend legitimacy to that game while our capacity for our own game is repressed and handicapped. To compete with the screech of the buzzards, canaries would have to forget their own warble and take singing lessons from their masters. Buzzards would always win.

The dominant totality always wins when the marginalized and oppressed communities compete among themselves for the status of "oppressed number one," that is, for the claim to represent the main paradigm of oppression, the root cause of suffering in the world, of which all other suffering is epiphenomenal. To be number one is the obsession of the powerful. To compete to be number one is to play the monological game that keeps the dominant totality together.

A methodological premise common to all liberation theologies is that no theological production is free from the mediations of its socio-historical locations. In other words theologians and communities of faith can think theologically only from within their specific contexts. To claim otherwise is to indicate methodological affinity with a monistic epistemology that seeks legitimacy in the idealistic language of universal premises and norms. This very claim to universality, however, is perceived by the marginalized communities as a tool of domestication used by the dominant center against the emergent struggles of the peripheries.

Liberation theologies, therefore, have broken away from idealistic epistemology; their multidisciplinary methodologies are informed not only by social philosophies but also by the social sciences, alternative memories, and other sources. From this perspective, monological claims not only are passé but represent a political agenda, an agenda that also can be named and brought to the level of formal articulation. The critical issue is not whether a given theology is political or not but what type of politics is concealed or revealed in its structure. The critical issue is whether one's community of accountability is a marginalized and oppressed group or the dominant center.

In some cases people are accountable to more than one community. This happens with black women, Hispanic women, Latin American women, Latin American blacks, and others. Recent developments in Latin American liberation theology illustrate this experience. Women like Elza Tamez, Ivone Gebara, Tereza Cavalcanti, and others are producing a distinctive brand of reflection in Latin America (see Tamez 1986). Their reflection is challenging male elements in Latin American theology as well as some premises of Anglo North American feminism. The same is true of the contributions of Latin American blacks to Latin American liberation theology. Quince Duncan, Laenne Hurbon, Eugenia Gonçalves, Joaquim Beato, and so many others are working on liberation theology from the perspective of blacks in Latin America (see Duncan et al. 1986). A challenge posed by both Latin American women and Latin American blacks to their North American sisters and brothers is a more intentional use of class analysis in theological reflection.

## LANGUAGES OF SOLIDARITY

The emerging dialogue between liberation theologies is a difficult one: How can the sociopolitical and economic liberation of Latin America help the struggles of North American women, blacks, and Hispanics? Aren't these struggles even antithetical to one another? What do North American women, blacks, and Hispanics have to gain with the economic and sociopolitical liberation of Latin America? Obviously this question can be reversed in many ways, and one can ask, What does black theology have to offer to feminism? Or, What does feminism have to offer to the liberation of the black community?

The search for common ground, however, does not imply that liberation theologies have to become a monological language. The premise that theology has to be a monological game is a key rule of the dominant theological discourse, which the marginalized communities—informed by their alternative memories and methods—have rejected.

Is solidarity then possible?

Yes and no. Solidarity is a hope for the struggle, but it is also a hope we need to struggle for. The challenge to the oppressed communities in struggle for solidarity is to find or invent new discursive paradigm(s) consistent with both their irreducible mutual challenges as well as common agenda. They need to replace the Hegelian monological dialectic (in which to each thesis a new antithesis emerges) with a dialogical one in which to each thesis many valid antitheses are possible. Only such a dialectic can sustain in dialogue the plurality of discourses needed in the struggle for solidarity.

Solidarity presumes distinction. As parrots and peacocks reject the buzzards' taste for carrion, they also reject the buzzards' presumption that their tastes are the best for everybody. Canaries will be happy with their gift for poetry; peacocks will be proud of their gift for colors; and they will not—like their teachers—conclude that everybody has to become a copy of themselves. Solidarity at this level means renouncing all interference in one another's projects. It is a negative solidarity in that it negates the imperialistic worldview of the dominant system. In practice, this is a solidarity of noninterference.

But theology is language (*theos-logos*, God-talk), and language is a technology of interference (McLuhan 1965, 57). With our languages we define the world around us, we define ourselves, and we even define the divine. Our definitions set the limits of what can or cannot be said (and thought) about anything (Merton 1967, 145). Languages, like games, have their own rules (Wittgenstein, 27–28). In a poker game, cards are handled differently from the way they are handled in a game of hearts—the same cards. Theologies of liberation are specific language games. Even though a substantial common ground exists between North American black theology and Latin American liberation theology, for example, not all their rules are the same. These communities think theologically from different social locations; they have alternative collective memories and so forth.

Solidarity also presumes common ground. A Latin American poet has suggested that the oppressed meet in the human body (Lima 1988,

103–4): The body of the wage worker is subjected to the military-like discipline of the industrial machine; the body of blacks is repressed because of its skin pigmentation; women are female bodies, oppressed as such. To this list of oppressed bodies one could add the very young (deprived of parental tenderness in collective socialization by day-care centers); the very old (confined to nursing homes by their yuppie children who grew up deprived of parental tenderness); gays and lesbians (repressed because of the drives of their bodies); the physically challenged (left out because of the accidents of their hurting bodies); and many others.

A hurting body has been the symbol of solidarity for Christians since the institution of the Holy Communion: "This is my body, . . . This is my blood." The celebration of this body was perceived as a threat to the status quo, the Roman totality, and so became a *sacramentum,* that is, an underground encounter in which people made and renewed their solidarity with each other unto death. This volume is a conversation among marginalized voices plotting together alternative worldviews, telling one another their forgotten dreams, and searching for ways to overcome the monological totality of the status quo with a practice and a language of mutual affirmation.

## CONFLICTS AND CONTEXTS

This work is divided into two parts: "Struggle and Solidarity" and "Disciplines in Dialogue."

In the first part we are introduced to the dilemmas posed by the challenge of solidarity to five paradigms of liberation theologies: Latin American (José Míguez Bonino), North American Black (James Cone), feminist (Rosemary Radford Ruether), Hispanic (Orlando Costas), and post-Holocaust/self-critical Jewish theology (Marc Ellis).

Míguez Bonino proposes a language that points to the structural connections between the many "dimensions of oppression" while avoiding a simplistic reduction of any one of these dimensions.

James Cone deals with solidarity as "an imperative and a dilemma" that has marked North American Black theology from the moment it was born, a child of the dialectical interaction between the civil rights movement (a movement of solidarity) and the Black Power movement (a movement of self-assertion and confrontation).

Rosemary Radford Ruether addresses questions of solidarity and conflict among women divided by different cultural and class experiences and backgrounds but unified by the experience of marginalization by patriarchy in the name of religion.

Orlando Costas presents the North American Hispanic perspective. A community marginalized by loss of territory to Anglo America, Hispanics bring to the North American cultural environment an alternative worldview in their bilingualism and repressed memories. Costas calls for a coherent articulation of the Hispanic explosive input and a constructive critical dialogue with other theologies in the Americas.

Marc Ellis represents yet another community whose voice has been a challenge to the status quo. His Jewish theology of liberation draws on both the ancient biblical prophetic tradition and modern scholarship, while transcending both, especially in its criticism of the so-called Holocaust theology—as represented by writers like Elie Wiesel, Emil Fackenheim, and Richard Rubenstein.

In the second section we are introduced to a range of issues and disciplines that occupy the agendas of liberation theologies—in dialogue.

Richard Shaull, a former Presbyterian missionary to Latin America and one of the forerunners of liberation theology, writes about the missionary/ministerial vocation of the church from the perspective of the new church emerging in the base communities of Latin America.

Harvey Cox's chapter on the silencing of Leonardo Boff is an examination of how the Sacred Congregation for the Doctrine of the Faith (of the Vatican) deals with indigenous contextualization of the Christian faith.

Pablo Richard develops a method of hermeneutics that affirms, on the one hand, both the ownership of the oppressed communities over their faith and its interpretation and, on the other hand, the input of the biblical sciences. These two theses are complementary, since one major insight of contemporary scientific biblical studies is that all biblical interpretations (even within the sacred text itself) belong to specific communities that find in the text clues to life's questions. Other insights from the biblical sciences are also crucial for the appropriation of the text by the oppressed communities, especially the tools to identify what Richard, following Carlos Mesters, calls the "corruptions of the text."

Otto Maduro's chapter is a sociological analysis of the religious conflict between Roman Catholic social teaching and Marxist theory.

Peter Paris first offers a description of the particular agendas of the major streams of liberation theologies and how their ethical reflections are articulated in terms of those agendas. He then adds to the current debate over liberation ethics his own reflection on the analytic paradigms of liberation theologies, their critique of ethics, the problem of conflict among oppressed groups, the problem of violence, and the primacy of justice as a theological principle.

The final two chapters engage contemporary literature in theological reflection. Lorine Getz uncovers a whole range of theological understandings on the relationship between nature and grace in the liberation stories of three women belonging to three different ethnic and racial communities in the Americas. The identification of these theological assumptions—not yet formally addressed by theological community— holds helpful keys to furthering dialogue among these groups.

Rubem Alves finds liberation theology in a text of Gabriel García Márquez. In it, beauty is a dance of symbols that tells the story of a poor fishing village, forgotten at the end of the world, that is resurrected by the appearance of a dead body on its shores.

## References

Alves, Rubem. 1984. *Estórias de Quem Gosta de Ensinar*. São Paulo: Cortez Editora and Editora Autores Associados.

Bingemer, Clara, et al. 1986. *El Rostro Feminino de la Teologia*. San José: Editorial DEI.

Duncan, Quince, et al. 1986. *Cultura Negra y Teologia*. San José: Editorial DEI.

Durkheim, Emile. [1915], 1965. *The Elementary Forms of Religious Experience*. New York: Free Press.

Dussel, Enrique. 1977. *Para Una Etica de la Liberacion Latinoamericana*, vols. 1– 5. Mexico: Editorial Edicol.

Huizinga, Johan. 1970. *Homo Ludens*. New York: Harper & Row.

Lima, Jr., José. 1988. *Corpoética: Cosquinhas Filosóficas no Umbigo da Utopia*. São Paulo: Paulinas.

Mannheim, Karl. 1953. Competition as a Cultural Phenomenon. In *Essays on the Sociology of Knowledge and Psychology*. Ed. Paul Kecskemeti. New York: Oxford Univ.

Marcuse, Herbert. 1968. *One Dimensional Man*. Boston: Beacon Press.

McLuhan, Marshall. 1965. *Understanding Media: The Extensions of Man*. New York: McGraw Hill.

Merton, Robert. 1967. *On Theocratic Sociology*. New York and London: Free Press.

Tamez, Elsa, ed. 1986. *Téologos de la Liberacion Hablan de la Mujer*. San José: Editorial DEI.

Wittgenstein, Ludwig. 1958. *The Blue and Brown Books*. Oxford: Blackwell.

# PART ONE

# STRUGGLE AND SOLIDARITY

# 1

# The Dimensions
# of Oppression

## José Míguez Bonino

───

"There are several theologies of liberation—which one will you be talking about?" This question can be asked from perplexity, concern, or hostility. It would be futile to claim precedence in time to establish one's own brand of liberation theology. In terms of content one would have to begin with the Old Testament and run the course of the whole history of the churches, where one would find different theologies of liberation or "ways of liberation" (Moltman 1974, 329–32). "Ah, that's because your theologies are contextual!" you naturally respond. But so is yours and everybody else's. The only questions are, How do you relate to the context, and how does your context relate to you? That is, From where do you interpret reality, and how does reality shape your interpretation? Is it possible to find unity in the so-called theologies of liberation, and is it possible to account for diversity within that unity? Is there a common "where from" of the interpretation and a common contextual conditioning? This chapter suggests some ways to look at this question.

## LIBERATION/OPPRESSION

It seems evident that we talk of liberation because we have some awareness—lesser or greater—of oppression. Things are not right as they are; at least they are not right for us. Those for whom things are

27

perfectly "all right"—an integrated cosmos of personal, social, and natural reality where everything fits perfectly—would not develop a reflection about liberation. A reflection about liberation, however, can only exist where the awareness of oppression is coupled with an awareness of the possibility of freedom from oppression—a hope, a dream, a restlessness, an expectation that things as they are ought to and can be changed. Which one of these two sides appears first is a matter for discussion. What seems clear is that both together are the presuppositions for a reflection about liberation. For that reflection to be a theology there must be in it a reference to a transcendent dimension. In other words the idea is that God is interested in oppression and liberation and, therefore, that a relation to that God has to do with the way we think and act in relation to oppression and liberation.

This still makes for a large and nebulous delineation. We cannot be satisfied with speaking in such terms. Our personal and collective experiences are encompassed by and inserted into this world. And we are people who confess the God who has come and who comes to us in Jesus Christ and the Spirit. Thus we talk about the relation between that God and our concrete experiences of oppression and liberation. We circumscribe the question to this time and this world. As we do so, we take account of the fact that some groups of people are actually acting and thinking from specific insights about God-oppression-liberation. Moreover, these groups are not disconnected: We have an experience of a conversation, a discussion, and an understanding but also of conflicts among these different groups. The experiences of Detroit in 1975, of Tanzania in 1976, of Geneva in 1983, of the Ecumenical Association of Third World Theologians are concrete data for our dialogue and reflection today.

## MULTIDIMENSIONAL EXPRESSION OF OPPRESSION/LIBERATION

As a way of concretizing our thinking, let us characterize broadly these different experiences and reflections, appropriating some insights from feminist, black, and Asian perspectives. I do so quite aware that I look at them from my own point of view, and therefore I stand ready to be challenged and corrected. But I do so also within the history of the relations, agreements, and disputes that have surfaced in it.

In *Household of Freedom* Letty Russell says, "Whatever feminist theologians take up transforms itself into an authority problem" (1986,

12). In a patriarchal society women experience oppression as domination, which means a loss of dignity, the sense of inferiority and worthlessness, the alienation of their identities. This experience makes it possible to discover patriarchy as a paradigm to understand the meaning and exercise of authority-as-domination that pervades the whole fabric of a society. In this sense "patriarchy is descriptive of every form of exploitation, not just sexism" (Russell 1986, 34). When Russell reads Scripture from this experience, she finds in it—side by side with this paradigm of domination—another understanding and exercise of authority as cooperation (empowering, authorizing), which she represents with the metaphor of the household. Liberation is seen as the construction of this new way of being human and of organizing the world. It holds not only for interpersonal, family, and church relations, but it is also a way of mending the world. It corresponds to health in the political and economic relations to which it alludes, for instance, in the biblical image of jubilee. Thus the experience of "the household of bondage" and the vision of "the household of freedom" born from the suffering and the hope of the women's struggle against sexism and male oppression result in a holistic approach to the liberation of all humankind and of creation.

The statement entitled *Challenge to the Church: A Theological Comment on the Political Crisis in South Africa*, now known as the *Kairos Document*, characterizes the South African situation as "a situation of death" but also as a *kairos* of judgment and opportunity "as the people refused to be oppressed or to cooperate with oppressors" (1985, i). The theologies of the state and the churches fail to face the challenge because they distort the biblical message. In the case of the state, they support their oppressive interests. In the case of the churches, they empty the biblical concepts of peace and reconciliation of their prophetic force. Then the authors of the document try to examine the nature of the situation of death. Black South African theology has been deeply aware of the racial nature of oppression. It is through racism that oppression was introduced, justified, and perpetuated. Liberation, therefore, had to be a reappreciation of their race, a vindication of the full dignity of blackness. The *Kairos Document* tries to enlarge this basic affirmation by relating racial oppression to the total system of death.

> It would be quite wrong to see the present conflict as simply a racial war. The racial component is there but we are not dealing with two equal races or nations each with their own selfish group interest. The situation we are dealing with here is one of oppression. (1985, 15)

Then they speak of the interests of the white minority, for whom the black people are mere labor units for the benefit of a privileged minority.

Korean Christian theologians have developed what is called Minjung theology. It builds on the opposition of "the people" as the oppressed over against the "oppressor," powerful and dominating (whether external or internal to the nation). But these Korean theologians strongly refuse to reduce this distinction to the economic level. "The proletariat is defined socio-economically," says Kim Yong Bock, "while the *minjung* is known politically" (Bock 1981, 186). What he means by political is the unity of the objective and the subjective conditions of a people that builds in history an identity not limited to any single aspect of the people—racial, economic—but expressed in their protest, their rebellion, their art and lore, their total attitude toward life, their myths and dreams. When they use the word *Han*—sigh, cry, protest—to characterize that subjectivity, they discover in it the secret of the persistence and the power that resides in this living identity. Messianism, the liberating counterface of the protest, is the people's way of assuming their identity as a mission of liberation.

In these brief references I am not trying to summarize feminist, black, South African, or Minjung theologies. I am simply trying to point out the fact that, from the perspective of their singular experiences, they are all led to expand the meaning of their categories in order to relate them to the totality of oppression and the struggle for liberation. Not by departing from their uniqueness or by diluting it into abstract categories but by deepening their particularity, they move toward universality. Variety is not an obstacle to unity but the way to it. It is not by denying feminist, black, or the Minjung experience or by treating them as epiphenomena of something else that we can find the way to commonality and solidarity. Is it possible to arrive at a theoretical formulation that will do justice to this insight?

## A THEORETICAL MODEL

Is there really a need for this theoretical model? Should we not be satisfied with the evident empathy and sympathy that exists between these different theologies and let each one pursue its particular struggle? I do not think so. Our sympathy and empathy must be made operative in history lest they become a purely idealistic construction. To do so we need an understanding on the basis of which a related number of practices may be built. Such a model will inevitably move at a level of abstraction. It cannot be a substitute for the particular experiences, nor can it replace the specific struggles. But if it really abstracts from concrete experience and praxis, it can give coherence to this diversity in a world in which we are irreversibly thrown together.

I am using as a model a scheme suggested by Enrique Dussel. Dussel suggests two axes in the reality of oppression: structural and ideological. He represents the first as a vertical line and the second as a horizontal line. The vertical axis relates two dimensions of oppression. One is economic—the expropriation of work, wealth, land, and economic space on the part of the oppressor and economic dependence on the part of the oppressed. The other dimension on the vertical axis is institutional and legal: the set of institutions and the body of laws that organize and regulate oppression, making it an order. It is not difficult to locate on one end of the axis women's work, worker's exploitation, slave labor, colonialism and neocolonialism, imperialism in different forms, and expropriation of the land from the peasants. On the other end of this axis are segregation laws, apartheid, unequal labor regulations for men and women, colonial laws, ethnic ghettos and reservations, colonial concessions, and much else.

On the horizontal axis we deal with phenomena of consciousness and their intellectual manifestations. At one end we have the image of the oppressed that the oppressors create for themselves (normally, subconsciously) in order to rationalize oppression and make it natural. In those pictures black and poor are lazy and passive, women are emotional and weak, certain peoples are benighted. Their cultural expressions, their social organizations, and their economic patterns are consequently also inferior and destined to disappear. Domination becomes, therefore, a moral obligation, a necessary discipline for the welfare and progress of the dominated, a service rendered to them. This ideology impregnates the language, the social habits, and customs; it thus perpetuates itself and becomes second nature in the oppressors. They can no more think themselves out of it than they can jump out of their skin. But this subconsciously built ideology most often works itself out also in intellectual or rational explanations: theories of race, biological superiority and inferiority, people's psychologies, anthropological theories and even economic and political theories. In this way a whole universe is created that functions as *the* universe for the oppressors.

The consciousness of the oppressed, at the other end of the horizontal axis, is built in a dialectical relation to the universe and natural order of the oppressors. On the one hand, this order seems to be the only possible one; the one that is cogently structured forms the only basis on which the oppressed can communicate—the language, the usages, the knowledge, indeed the very rationality into which they are socialized. On the other hand, their experience as oppressed contradicts the rationality of that universe. Frequently, the oppressed are simultaneously socialized into a different language, different usages and symbols, a different wisdom that is the common patrimony of the oppressed and that is at odds with the universe of the oppressors. The consciousness of the oppressed is thus a split one, made of adaptation and discomfort, of acquiescence and revolt. Such contradiction seldom finds expression in an articulated intellectual system, but it is reflected in popular art and music, in messianic movements, and in the stories of the people. Sometimes an intellectual, a person organically related to the oppressed, finds a way to elaborate these insights and experiences and to delineate a project that challenges the induced submission of the masses. These expressions of the protest and rebellion by the oppressed have repercussions in the world of the oppressors, disturbing their ideologically self-assured consciousness, revealing the artificiality of their constructed universe, and introducing a crisis.

Religion participates in the four foci I described above. In relation to slavery or the institutionalization in the churches of class division, religion clearly participates in economic oppression and exploitation. Caste systems, segregation laws and segregated churches, proscriptions of women by church law from functions and offices—all can be found in the history of all religions. There is no doubt, however, that the expression of oppression/liberation is preeminently religious at the level of the formation of consciousness, since religion usually provides the symbolic representations that cement a people's (class's, group's, societies') conception of the world and of themselves in it. Since religion represents an ultimate commitment, it plays a fundamental role in the formation of consciousness. It gives transcendent legitimacy to a given order—a legitimacy that, as the virulence of religious conflicts today shows, continues to be important even in "secularized" societies.

Religion provides "wholeness" to the consciousness of the oppressors. But perhaps its main function is in the introjection of oppression among the oppressed. It functions as an instrument of domination by creating in the oppressed a "religious" acceptance of domination as a sacred duty and even as a means of salvation. The religion of the oppressed, like their consciousness, is split. The sense of protest, of the inadequacy between the transcendent power and the conditions in which they live, finds expression in prayer, myth, song, and the creation of their own pantheon. This ambiguity of religion as the privileged instrument of ideological domination, but also as the place where the split in consciousness finds the deepest expression, makes religion an important field in the struggle for liberation.

## CONSEQUENCES OF THE MODEL

This theoretical model points to three consequences:

First, for different groups of people, the awareness of oppression focuses at one point in this spectrum of oppression, and consequently the struggle for liberation concentrates around this focus. It seems in feminist movements, for instance, that at early stages the focus is on juridical and institutional levels (women's vote, access to public functions or professional education and work), and later it moved to the whole consciousness problem (self-criticism for accepting the male image of femininity; denunciation of the patriarchal ideology of domination; and struggle for inclusive language). Of course, the institutional front continues alongside this new one. Occasionally one finds, as for instance in Dorothee Soelle's correlation of objective and subjective cynicism, a substantial discussion of the economic dimension.

Black liberation thinking seems to have followed a similar pattern in the struggle for civil rights, on the one hand, and the vindication of blackness, on the other. In the exploration of their rich cultural past they found a point of rupture with the oppressors at the level of consciousness, which frequently became an open rebellion. The very nature of black experience, both in the Americas and in Africa, has brought economic oppression to figure prominently in black thinking.

Latin American theology of liberation was led from the beginning to see economic exploitation (dependence in international terms and class exploitation both internally and externally) as its fundamental category. Liberation for the poor, which cannot take place without a change in the economic system, has also meant a political transformation. In the course of the last twenty years that focus has not changed. But the deepening of reflection and experience in the life of the liberation movements have made clear that the economic-political dimension cannot be isolated from other factors. The political, however, does not, by itself, exhaust the meaning of oppression. Class characterizations are supplemented by more fluid ones like "the poor," "the nonperson," "the underside of history," "cultural impoverishment," "anthropolog-ical poverty" (as some African theologians call it), ethnic factors, the condition of women, and spirituality. They have all become important elements in understanding oppression and in the struggle for liberation. Thus one important fact for the relation of theologies of liberation is this: The point of departure of an awareness of oppression and a struggle for liberation can take place anywhere in this wide spectrum (economic, institutional, juridical, cultural, religious), but, if pursued in depth and extension, one will lead to the others.

The second point, at this time an unresolved question, refers to the first. Are these different instances of oppression and liberation inde-pendent of each other or are they reflections of one another? We cannot yet give a definitive answer to this long-debated question. But our experience in the struggle for liberation is enough to make two asser-tions. First, there is a clear interconnection between these different aspects—objective and subjective, economic and sociopolitical. They impinge on each other and mutually condition each other. Second, each one of them has a certain autonomy and cannot be simply reduced to a mechanical effect of another. To respect the autonomy and to discern the interconnection of these different dimensions are urgent tasks for liberation thinking. This relative autonomy demands from the theo-logian the use of a number of human sciences as mediation: those that explore the social and economic structure of society, where Marxism plays an important role, and those related to subjectivity, identity, and meaning (hermeneutical sciences, anthropology, ethnology, linguistics, psychology). This means that theology can today be done only as an interdisciplinary exercise.

The theoretical model also points to a third consequence. In the present movement toward an ever more interrelated world, oppressions experienced in so many different ways are integrated into one oppres-sion—a system of death that operates everywhere, at every level of life. This is not to speak of some "conspiracy theory" (although some co-inspiration exists) but of objective structures of power and of a cor-respondent rationality that drive toward globalizing oppression. Each struggle for liberation, without giving up or minimizing its localized engagement, needs to relate to this total system and to this common struggle. To do so we need to analyze together, not only the way in which theologies supplement and reinforce each other, but also how the total context feeds into particular struggles and how this latter fits into the struggle for a new world order. An exclusive, piecemeal ap-proach may play into the hands of the total system of oppression.

## References

Bock, Kim Yong, ed. 1981. *Minjung Theology*. Singapore: Commission on Theological Education.

*Challenge to the Church: A Theological Comment on the Political Crisis in South Africa.* 1985. South Africa: Kairos Theologians. (Known as the *Kairos Document.*)

Dussel, Enrique. 1979. Racismo, America Latina negra y teologia de la liberacion. Unpublished paper presented in Jamaica (December 27–30).

Moltmann, Jürgen. 1974. *The Crucified God*. New York: Harper & Row.

Russell, Letty M. 1986. *Household of Freedom: Authority in Feminist Theology.* Philadelphia: Westminster Press.

Soelle, Dorothee. 1980. *Choosing Life*. Philadelphia: Fortress Press.

# 2

# Black Theology and the Imperative and Dilemma of Solidarity

## James H. Cone

Black theology was conceived by Black Christians in the United States as an expression of hope and as a tool of struggle for liberation. From the moment of its conception, Black theology has been energized by the tension that made it possible and necessary: on the one hand, the Christian dream of the "beloved community" as expressed by Martin Luther King, Jr., and on the other hand, the transformation of the American dream into a nightmare for Blacks, as Malcolm X claimed. The roots of Black theology go back to the experience of faith and the struggles of our first forebears. My reflection here on the dilemma posed by solidarity among liberation theologies starts with Black theology as it emerged in the context of the civil rights movement of the 1950s and 1960s, largely associated with Martin Luther King, Jr., and the rise of the Black Power movement, strongly influenced by Malcolm X.

## THE EMERGENCE OF BLACK THEOLOGY

The communities involved in the rise of Black theology were also involved in the civil rights movement, and they participated in the protest demonstrations led by Martin Luther King, Jr. Unlike most contemporary theological movements in Europe and North America,

Black theology's birthplace was not the seminary or university. In fact most of the early interpreters of Black theology did not have advanced academic degrees. Black theology came into being in the context of Black people's struggle for racial justice, which was instituted in the church but chiefly identified with such protest organizations as the Southern Christian Leadership Conference (SCLC), the National Conference of Black Christians (NCBC), the Inter-Religion Foundation for Community Organization (IFCO), and many Black caucuses in White denominations.

From the beginning Black theology was understood by its creators as a Christian theological reflection upon Black struggles for justice and liberation. This was defined largely by Martin Luther King, Jr., when he and other Black church people began to relate the gospel to the struggle for justice in North American society. The majority of White theologians denied any relationship between the Black struggle for justice and the gospel. They claimed that politics and religion did not mix. Liberal White Christians, with few exceptions, remained silent on the theme of justice or advocated a form of gradualism that denounced boycotts, sit-ins, and freedom rides. Contrary to popular opinion, King was not well received by the White American church establishment when he inaugurated the civil rights movement with the Montgomery bus boycott in 1955.

Because Black people received no support from White churches or their theologians, we had to search deeply in our own history to find the theological basis for our political commitment to set Black people free. We found support in people like Richard Allen, who in response to White segregation founded the African Methodist Episcopal (AME) church; in Henry Highland Garnet, a nineteenth-century Presbyterian preacher who urged slaves to resist slavery; in Nat Turner, a slave and Baptist preacher who led an insurrection that killed sixty Whites; in Harriet Tubman, a runaway slave who led more than three hundred slaves to freedom; in Sojourner Truth, an ex-slave who became a prominent speaker against slavery and for women's rights; and in Henry McNeal Turner, an AME bishop who claimed that God was a Negro. When we investigated our religious history, we were reminded that our struggle for political justice did not begin in the 1950s or 1960s, but had roots stretching back for many decades.

It was encouraging to find out that Black people's struggle for political justice in North America has always been located in their churches. Black Christians have always known that the God of Moses and Jesus did not create them to be slaves or second-class citizens to Whites. This conviction is found throughout the Black church experience—whether we consider (1) the independent churches, such as the AME, AME Zion, and Baptist; (2) the so-called invisible institutions among the slaves in the South, which merged with the independent churches after the Civil War; or (3) Black people in White organizations. To make a theological witness of this religious knowledge, Black preachers and civil rights activists of the 1960s developed a Black theology that rejected racism and affirmed the Black struggle for liberation as consistent with the gospel of Jesus.

After the march on Washington in August 1963, the integration theme in the Black community began to lose ground to the Black nationalist philosophy of Malcolm X. Riots in the ghettos of U.S. cities were shocking evidence that many Blacks agreed with Malcolm's contention that America was not a dream but a nightmare. It was not until the summer of 1966, however, after Malcolm's assassination, that the term *Black Power* began to be used. The occasion was the continuation of the James Meredith "march against fear" in Mississippi. After James Meredith was shot during the first part of the march, King, Stokely Carmichael, Floyd McKissick, and other civil rights activists took up the leadership. Stokely Carmichael seized this occasion to sound the Black Power slogan, and it was heard loud and clear throughout the United States. The rise of Black Power had a profound effect upon the appearance of Black theology. When Carmichael and other Black activists separated themselves from King's absolute commitment to nonviolence by proclaiming Black Power, White church people called upon their Black brothers and sisters in the gospel to denounce the Black Power slogan as un-Christian. To the surprise of White Christians, Black ministers refused to follow their advice. Instead they wrote a Black Power statement that was published in the *New York Times* on July 31, 1966. The appearance of this statement may be regarded as the beginning of the conscious development of a Black theology by Black ministers. It was in these two contexts, the civil rights movement and the Black Power movement, that Black theology emerged.

Many White Christians and almost all White theologians dismiss Black theology as nothing but rhetoric. Since White theologians control the seminaries and the university departments of religion, they try to make Black people feel that only Europeans (and people who think like them) can define theology. To challenge the White monopoly on the definition of theology, many young Black scholars realized that they had to carry the fight to the seminaries and the universities where theology was being written and taught. In 1969 I wrote the first book on Black theology, entitled *Black Theology and Black Power*. Its central thesis was the identification of the liberating elements in Black Power with the Christian gospel. One year later I authored *A Black Theology of Liberation*. This book made liberation the organizational center of my theological perspective. I wrote, "Christian theology is a theology of liberation, it is *a rational study of the being of God in the world, in the light of an existential situation of an oppressed community struggling for freedom, relating the forces of liberation to the essence of the Gospel which is Jesus Christ*" (17).

After these works appeared, other Black theologians joined me, supporting my theological project but challenging what they regarded as my theological excesses. For example, J. Deotis Roberts published in 1971 *Liberation and Reconciliation*, which supported my emphasis on liberation but claimed that I overlooked reconciliation as central to the gospel and to Black-White relations. A similar position was advocated by Major Jones in *Black Awareness: A Theology of Hope*, published in 1971. Other Black theologians, including Cecil Cone in his 1971 work, claimed that I was too dependent on White theology and not sufficiently aware of the African origins of Black religion. This same criticism is found in Gayraud Wilmore's book, *Black Religion and Black Radicalism*.

Though my perspective on Black theology was and continues to be challenged by other Black scholars, they support my claim that liberation was the central core of the gospel as found in the Scriptures and in the religious history of Black Americans. For Black theologians the political meaning of liberation was best illustrated in the Exodus, and its future or eschatological meaning was found in the life, death, and resurrection of Jesus. The Exodus was interpreted as analogous to Nat Turner's slave insurrection and Harriet Tubman's liberation of an estimated three hundred slaves. The slave songs (often called Negro spirituals), sermons, and prayers expressed the eschatological character of liberation found in the resurrection of Jesus.

More recently Womanist theology has emerged as an open challenge to the current patriarchal character of Black theology. The writings of Jacquelyn Grant, Clarice Martin, Delores Williams, Katie G. Cannon, Kelly D. Brown, Cheryl Gilkes, and Renita Weems are examples of this emerging theology. While the proponents of Womanist theology accept the liberation theme of Black theology, they reject its narrow limitations to racism—as if sexism were not also an important problem in the Black community. Because of the urgency of the problem of sexism, Black women have begun to insist on doing theology out of their experience. They have introduced the theme of *survival* as a necessary compliment of the idea of liberation. No community can be liberated if it does not survive. Hagar, the slave woman, not Moses, the liberator, is the key biblical person who influenced the development of Womanist theology. Womanist theology is both a challenge to the sexist orientation of Black male theology and a deepening of the struggle against racism.

## BLACK AND THIRD WORLD THEOLOGIES

The challenge for Black theology to appreciate a larger definition of liberation also comes from contact with other forms of liberation theology in Africa, Latin America, and Asia. Black theology in South Africa is a natural ally. Black and Latin American theologies became partners in their identification of the gospel with the liberation of the poor, although Black theology has emphasized racism and Latin American theology has emphasized classism. A similar partnership has taken place with African and Asian theologians regarding the importance of culture in the definition of theology.

In a continuing dialogue with third world theologians, the striking difference between the theologies of the poor and the theologies of the rich has become clear. Dialogue helped us move beyond our earlier critique, which had been confined to North American racism. African, Asian, and Latin American theologians enlarged our vision by challenging us to do theology from a perspective of global oppression. Third world theologians urged us to analyze racism in relation to international capitalism, imperialism, colonialism, world poverty, classism, and sexism.

For the first time Black theologians began to consider socialism as an alternative to capitalism. We began to see the connection between Black ghettos in the United States and poverty in Africa, Asia. and Latin America; between the rise in unemployment among Blacks and other poor people in the United States and exploitation of third world peoples; between the racist practices of White churches from North America and Europe and their missionaries in the third world. These discoveries deeply affected our political and theological vision. We began to see clearly that we could not do theology in isolation from the struggle of our brothers and sisters in the third world. As oppressors have banded together to keep the poor of the world in poverty, so the world's poor must enter into political and theological solidarity to create a movement of liberation that is capable of breaking the chains of oppression.

Early in the dialogue, Black and third world theologians realized the importance of building a common movement of liberation. Although we experienced differences among ourselves, our mutual commitment to do theology in solidarity with the poor held us together. We had too much in common to allow our differences to separate us. Furthermore it became increasingly apparent that our differences were largely due to a difference in our contexts and to our internalization of the lies that our oppressors had told us about each other. After nearly eight years of dialogue under the Ecumenical Association of Third World Theologians, our differences have diminished considerably and our similarities have increased to the extent that we are now engaged in the exciting task of attempting to create a third world theology of liberation that we all can support.

When the question is asked, How do we do theology? Black and third world theologians agree that theology is not the first act of the religious community but rather the second. Although our Latin American brothers and sisters were the first explicitly to use the Marxist concept of praxis, it was already present in all our theologies and now has been reaffirmed. So the first act is both a religiocultural and a political commitment on behalf of the poor and baseless.

Our cultural identity and political commitment are worth more than a thousand textbooks of theology. That is why we do not talk about theology as the first order of business in our association. Rather our first concern is with the quality of commitment that each of us has made and will make for those about whom and with whom we claim to do theology. We contend that we know what people believe by what they do and not by what they say in their creeds, conference statements, or theological textbooks. Praxis comes before theology in any formal sense.

Our reason for doing theology arises out of our experiences in the ghettos, the villages, and the churches of the poor in our countries. We do not believe it necessary for our people to remain poor. Something must be done about their misery. Because the starting point of our theologies is defined by a prior affirmation of and political commitment to be in solidarity with the poor, our theologies bear the names that reflect our affirmations and commitments. We call our theologies Black, African, Hispanic-American, Asian, Red, Latin American, Womanist, and a host of other names that sound strange to people whose theological knowledge has been confined to European and White North American theologies. The identities of our theologies are determined by the human and the divine dimensions of reality to which we bear witness.

We do not begin our theology with a reflection on divine revelation, as if the God of our faith is separate from the suffering of our people. We do not believe that revelation is a deposit of fixed doctrines or an objective word of God that is then applied to the human situation. On the contrary we contend that there is no truth outside of, or beyond, the concrete historical events in which our people are engaged. Truth, therefore, is found in the histories, the cultures and the religions of our peoples.

Our focus on social and religiocultural analysis separates our theological enterprise from the abstract theologies of Europe and North America. It also illuminates the reason why praxis, in contrast to orthodoxy, has become for many of us the criterion for doing theology. Although Black and third world theologians have been accused by European and North American critics of reducing theology to ideology, we contend that the criticism is misplaced. It camouflages the human character of all theologies, particularly the fact that our critics are doing theology from the perspective of the rich and powerful. Unlike our critics, we do not claim to be neutral in our theology. The enormity of the suffering of our people demands that we choose *for* their liberation and *against* the structures of oppression. We cannot let the people who support the structures of oppression define theology for us. Black theologians agree with Malcolm X: "Don't let anybody who's oppressing us ever lay down the ground rules. Don't go by their game, don't play by their rules. Let them know that this is a new game and we've got some new rules" (Malcolm X 1970, 155).

The dominant theologians in Europe and North America want to retain the current theological rules because they made them. Their rules help keep the world as it is: Whites dominating Blacks, men dominating women, and rich nations keeping poor nations dependent. But we are living in a new world situation and this new situation requires a new way of doing theology. Again Malcolm X expressed it:

> The time we are living in and are facing now is not an era where one who is oppressed is looking toward the oppressor to give him some system or form of logic or reason. What is logical to the oppressor isn't logical to the oppressed, and what is reason to the oppressor isn't reason to the oppressed. The Black people in this country are beginning to realize that what sounds

reasonable to those who exploit us doesn't sound reasonable to us. There just has to be a new system of reason and logic devised by us who are on the bottom, if we want some results in this struggle that is called the "Negro Revolution." (Epps 1968, 133)

In the Ecumenical Association of Third World Theologians, Black and third world theologians have been attempting to develop this new way of making theology. In contrast to the dominant theologies of Europe and North America that are largely defined by their responses to the Enlightenment and the problem of the unbeliever that arose from it, our theological enterprise focuses on Europe's and North America's invasion of the continents of Asia, Africa, and Latin America, inaugurating the slave trade, colonization, and neocolonialism.

Our primary theological question, therefore, is not how we can believe in God in view of modern Western confidence in science, reason, and technology, which seems to exclude the necessity of faith. Rather our primary theological question and problem arise from the encounter of God in the experience and misery of the poor. How can we speak about Jesus' death on the cross without first speaking about the death of poor people? How can the poor of our country achieve worth as human beings in a world that has attempted to destroy our cultures and our religions?

The chief issue of our theologies is the problem of the nonperson, the poor person. That is why our partners in the universities are not the philosophers, metaphysicians, and other socially disinterested intellectuals. Rather they are the social scientists and political activists concerned about and engulfed in the struggle for the liberation of the poor.

Black and third world theologians' concerns about the oppressed person forced us to establish links with the communities of the poor. In the ecclesial church life of these communities we have experienced something more than a routine gathering of like-minded people. In their worship life is revealed a knowledge of themselves that cannot be destroyed by the structures that oppress them. Their faith in God evolves out of their cultural and political aspirations. It can be observed in the basic communities of Latin America, the Black and Hispanic churches of North America, the indigenous churches and traditional religions of Africa, and the religious life of Asia. In their worship the God of grace and of judgment meets poor people and transforms their personhood from nobody to somebody and bestows upon them the power and the courage to struggle for justice and peace.

Worship, therefore, is not primarily an expression of the individual's private relationship to God. Rather it is a community happening, an eschatological invasion of God into the gathered community of victims, empowering them with the "divine spirit from on high" to "keep on keeping on," even though the odds might be against them. In the collective presence of the poor at worship, God recreates them as the liberated community who must now bring freedom to the oppressed of the land. Black and third world theologies are being created out of the poor people's church and religious life as they seek to interpret the God encountered in their religiocultural and political struggle to overcome European and U.S. domination.

## NEW VISIONS NEED NEW ANALYSIS

Where do we go from here? The spirituality of Black churches, creatively expressed in worship, and the Black theology emerging from it have been taken to many parts of the globe, strengthening the determination of the oppressed "to keep their faith in the God of justice," whose righteousness is always found in the liberation of the oppressed.

In Black religion, faith in the God of justice and the human struggle to implement it belong together and cannot be separated without both of them losing their authenticity. The faith of African-Americans is deeply embedded in our African and slave past. It has sustained our identity amid wretched circumstances, extending our spiritual and political vision far beyond the alternatives provided by the Whites who enslaved us.

Since 1955 the misery of the poor has increased to massive proportions in a world of plenty for a few. The widening gap between the rich and the poor and the real possibility of nuclear annihilation mean that we need to reevaluate our definition of freedom and the methods we have used to attain it. Is not a deeper analysis of our struggle required if we expect to achieve liberation for the poor and survival for all? When I evaluate the historical development of Black churches and the civil rights movement, as well as the theological and political reflection connected with them, I think we Blacks have a right to say that they have brought us "a mighty long way." But I am not sure that they will be able to take us much further if they do not lead to radical changes in our analysis of Black freedom and the methods we have used in our attempt to implement it.

We need a vision of freedom that includes the whole of the inhabited earth and not just Black North America, a vision enabling us to analyze the causes of world poverty and sickness, monopoly capitalism, and antidemocratic socialism; opium in Christianity and other religions among the oppressed, racism and sexism, and the irresolute will to eliminate these evils. We must analyze these complex and deeply rooted evils in such a manner that the Black struggle and faith can be seen as expressing solidarity with the struggles and faiths of others who are fighting for the liberation of the wretched of this earth.

Although I do not believe that Blacks will achieve full freedom through the election process, I want to emphasize that political action is a necessary step toward freedom. Unless the masses assume responsibility by voting, they will not be able to affect the political process. The freedom of our children and that of others is dependent upon our political engagement in the struggles for justice. To be a Christian is to love one's neighbor and that means making a political commitment to make the world a habitable place for one's neighbor. Christians are called not only to pray for justice but also to become actively involved in establishing it.

Black churches have a special responsibility for the world because we claim that Christ died to redeem it. When others give up in despair, feeling overwhelmed by the enormity of the evil that engulfs us, Black churches continue to preach hope because "when a people has no vision, it perishes."

Yet how can we sing "Glory Hallelujah" when our people's blood is flowing in the streets and prisons of this nation? What do we Blacks have to shout about when our families are being broken and crushed by political, social, and economic forces so complex that most of us do not know what to do to resist them? This is the paradox that makes faith necessary if we are to survive the oppression and do the analysis necessary to overcome it. To pray for justice without analyzing the causes of injustice is to turn religion into an opiate of the people. The time has come for the Black church to take a critical look at its vision with the intent of radically changing its priorities. We need to dream about new possibilities or our people will perish, not only from racism and capitalism but also from our own neglect and illusions.

The vision of a new social order should not be taken from any one person. The vision should be the result of a group of committed people whose love for freedom is deep and broad enough to embrace and consider many viewpoints. This would include a cross section of the total Black community, including community grass-roots activists and scholars, scientists and politicians, artists and lawyers, teachers and preachers, men and women, youth and senior citizens, Christians and non-Christians. The chief requirement should be commitment to the freedom of all. The initiative for the new vision and the creation of a team to help should come from the Black church. The financial resources for the program must come from the Black community. No oppressed people has ever had its freedom given as a gift or financed by its oppressor. Freedom must be taken, and it involves risk, struggle, and a commitment to stand against those who deny it.

The life and thought of Martin Luther King, Jr., and Malcolm X are the best examples in the Black community of the creative role that religion can play in the transformation of society. They combined their religious vision with their political commitment, but they refused to allow either their politics or their faith to separate them from other people struggling for justice even though those people held different views.

The creation of a just social order must be grounded in the hopes that have been engendered by the poor as they have emerged from their encounter with God in their fight for freedom. Thus the prereflective visions of the poor, as defined by their political struggles and celebrated in their religious life, must be taken seriously. Although I am a Christian theologian, I contend that a just social order must be accountable to not one but many religious communities. If we are going to create a society that is responsive to the humanity of all, then we must not view one religious faith as absolute. Ultimate reality, to which all things are subject, is too mysterious to be exclusively limited to one people's view of God. Any creation of a just social order must take into account that God has been known and experienced in many different ways. Because we have an imperfect grasp of divine reality, we must not regard our limited vision as absolute. Solidarity among all human communities is antithetical to religious exclusivism. God's truth comes in many colors and is revealed in many cultures, histories, and unexpected places. Because I am a Christian whose theological and political perspective has been defined by the Black church tradition, my view of a just social order cannot be understood apart from my faith in God's liberating presence in Jesus. The importance of God and Jesus for Black Christians is best explained when we consider the preponderance of suffering in Black life and Blacks' attempt to affirm their humanity in spite of it. We have survived slave ships, auction blocks, and chronic unemployment because the God of faith has bestowed upon us an identity that cannot be destroyed by White oppressors. No matter what trials and tribulations Blacks encounter, we refuse to let despair define our humanity. We simply believe that "God can make a way out of no way." The eschatological hope in Black faith is born of struggle here and now because Black Christians refuse to allow oppressors to define who we are.

## References

Cone, Cecil. 1971. *Identity Crisis in Black Theology*. Nashville: AMEC.

Cone, James. 1969. *Black Theology and Black Power*. New York: Seabury Press.

———. 1970. *A Black Theology of Liberation*. Philadelphia: Lippincott Press.

Epps, Archie, ed. 1968. *The Speeches of Malcolm X at Harvard*. New York: Morrow.

Jones, Major. 1971. *Black Awareness: A Theology of Hope*. Nashville: Abingdon Press.

Malcolm X. 1970. *By Any Means Necessary*. Ed. George Breitman. New York: Pathfinder.

Roberts, J. Deotis. 1971. *Liberation and Reconciliation*. Philadelphia: Westminster Press.

Wilmore, Gayraud. 1972. *Black Religion and Black Radicalism*. Maryknoll: Orbis Books.

# 3

# Feminist Theology and Interclass/Interracial Solidarity

## Rosemary Radford Ruether

In this reflection on feminist theology and solidarity between women across class, cultural, and racial lines, I am aware that feminist theology is increasingly entering into a pluralistic situation. Feminist theology, very appropriately, is manifesting itself as a multicontextual phenomenon. Christian women from many cultural contexts, both in the United States and internationally, are finding their own distinctive voice and perspective on feminist theology. Feminist theological or religious reflection is also emerging in various other religious traditions, such as Judaism, Buddhism, and Islam.

White Western Christian women in the United States who have pioneered much of the foundations of feminist theology need to become increasingly aware of this multicontextual expression of feminist religious reflection. They need to recognize their own feminist theology and hermeneutics as emerging from one social and cultural context among others, rather than implicitly assuming that their work is *the* feminist theology or is the normative feminist theological perspective. In short, the same critique of cultural imperialism that feminism has applied to white male theology needs also to be applied to white Western Christian feminist theology.

What is the basis for solidarity among feminist theologies across class, racial, and even religious lines? How can particular feminist theologies both relativize their own claims and also reach across the divisions of women into distinct communities of historical experience to

49

embrace a growing plurality of feminist religious reflection? I will begin here with intra-Christian solidarity and then reflect on solidarity across religious faith communities.

## SHARED HERITAGE, DIVERSE PRESENT

All Christian women, whether white, black, Asian, or Hispanic, whether working from a North American context or in Europe, Asia, Africa, or Latin America, have the same basic problems with Christian Scripture and tradition. The strictures in Scripture and historical tradition up until the seventeenth century against women preaching, leading congregations, or being ordained were directed against all women indiscriminately, not simply at poor or culturally disadvantaged women. Indeed privileged women of the same class and cultural group as the male elite were the most immediate target of these strictures, since they were the women most likely to be in a position to claim leadership roles.

Beginning in the seventeenth century with their endorsement of women's preaching and participation in church management, the Society of Friends began to forge a new tradition that was more inclusive of women. But even the Quakers tended to fall back into patterns of subordination of women, particularly in the social order. A few Christian groups began to ordain women in the second half of the nineteenth century. The major shift to ordination of women and inclusion of women in theological education preparatory to ordination among liberal Protestants began in 1956. But women even in these traditions do not face an unambiguous situation. Arguments continue to be made even in these traditions against women's ordination. Backlash groups, such as the authors of the Methodist Houston Statement, attempt to argue that inclusive language for God is heretical. Scripture binds Christians to male language for the Trinity, they claim.

Thus Christian women of all traditions, even those that ordain women, still face an androcentric and misogynist Christian past. A new hermeneutic and an inclusive theology have not yet emerged and been claimed as normative by their churches and by theological educators. Thus the work of feminist biblical hermeneutic and theological critique done by feminist scholars in a white Western context is relevant to all Christian women. All Christian women are confronted by much the same arguments from church authorities against their full inclusion in church leadership.

This does not mean that this hermeneutical work is fully adequate for women disprivileged by class and race. They may need to extend this scholarship to additional dimensions of the question of sexism not addressed by earlier feminist scholarship. For example, the question of how slavery interacts with the status of women in the Scriptures needs further development. Lesbian women will raise additional questions about heterosexist images of social hierarchy that have gone unnoticed in earlier feminist scholarship.

Each new community of women that gains its own distinctive voice opens up a rich new vein of critical work. The entire enterprise of feminist theological critique is thus enriched by these new insights. This does not mean that each community of feminist reflection remains limited to its own vantage point. Just as black, Hispanic, or Asian women took over and built on the work of Anglo-American women, so these women need to learn from the new insights of their black, Hispanic, and Asian sisters. A certain shared tradition of Christian feminist work needs to be built up through this dialogue and interchange.

Once problems of slavery and heterosexism, as part of the context of sexism in Hebrew Scripture and New Testament studies, have been pointed out by black or lesbian women, that needs to change the way all Christian feminists look at their work. Needless to say, feminists are making the same demands on male theologians and biblical scholars. Once the sexist issues have been pointed out, it becomes illegitimate for any Christian scholar to ignore these findings. A new shared Christian tradition for all Christians needs to be developed.

## JEWISH AND CHRISTIAN FEMINIST HERMENEUTICS

Somewhat different questions are posed by dialogue between Jewish and Christian women on scriptural hermeneutics. Christian and Jewish women share a common Scripture, Hebrew Scripture, authoritative for both traditions but in quite different ways and with different traditions of interpretation. Specifically, Christianity made nonnormative what is most normative for the Jewish tradition, namely, the Levitical tradition. Christianity uses the part of Hebrew Scripture that it claims as preparation for and prediction of Christ, a hermeneutic totally unacceptable to Judaism. Christian Scripture, the New Testament, is not normative for Jews. Moreover it enshrines the patterns of negation and supersession of Judaism that are the roots of Christian anti-Judaism.

Jewish and Christian women have hardly begun to dialogue on this fundamental conflict between the way their two traditions appropriate Scripture. Such dialogue as has developed between Jewish and Christian feminists has primarily taken the form of a Jewish feminist critique of unconscious patterns of anti-Judaism in Christian feminist hermeneutic. I believe the Christian feminists in the United States sincerely seek to hear this critique and to incorporate a sensitivity to it into their own work. But it is difficult for them to be aware of how deeply all their presuppositions are conditioned by anti-Judaism.

Also it is difficult to know where illegitimate anti-Judaism ends and legitimate critique of the sexism and other social deficiencies in Judaism begins. There is a Jewish joke that asks, "What is the difference between a prophet and an anti-Semite?" The answer: "The anti-Semite says, 'The Jews are terrible'; the prophet says, 'The Jews are terrible, oiiee!' " In other words, the prophet critiques the Jewish tradition from within, as one who identifies with it. The anti-Semite attacks it from without, as a tradition that he or she does not identify with and wishes to vilify. The same words take on entirely different meanings in the two contexts.

Clearly many of the criticisms of sexism that Christians might make about Hebrew Scripture or the early rabbinic tradition are the same criticisms that Jewish feminists would want to make. But when Christian feminists make these criticisms, they often sound anti-Semitic to Jews. This is because the Christian makes these criticisms from outside the Jewish tradition, from a context that makes these Jewish traditions nonnormative for Christians and that often implies that Christianity does not share these same problems. Thus it sounds as if Christianity is once again setting itself up as the salvific alternative to a flawed and superseded Judaism.

Christian and Jewish feminists have a long way to go before they can truly dialogue from their distinct traditions as peers. Yet Christian feminists need to learn from Jewish feminists not only about anti-Judaism but also how Jewish feminists interpret Scripture. Jewish feminists are just beginning to sort out their own distinct hermeneutical perspective for critique and interpretation of Scripture from a Jewish feminist context. This perspective needs to become a shared perspective for Jews and Christians, just as Jewish feminists have made critical use of Christian hermeneutics.

This question of moving from different and distinct perspectives to shared perspectives raises once again the difficult question of universalism and particularism. To what extent is it possible by combining these many perspectives, coming from various cultural and religious contexts, to work toward a universal perspective? My view is that a fully universal perspective will always elude us. No matter how many varieties of perspectives we attempt to include, we are still creating a larger, but finite, contextualization. We need to acknowledge the finitude and limits of any possible perspective.

The need to work toward inclusion of perspectives must distinguish, however, between questions of justice and questions of culture. Perspectives that enforce unjust stereotypes of other groups, that negate their fullness of humanity and access to the divine, and that marginalize their access to cultural resources, are morally wrong. One must seek a sensitivity to all such patterns of discrimination that overcomes such unjust discrimination. But there is the theoretically separable (although not easily separated) issue of distinctions of culture, which is morally neutral. Here cultural pluralism can be appreciated by others without any attempt to incorporate these other cultural perspectives into their own interpretation. An Anglo-American feminist might be enriched by an African feminist who incorporates African cultural material specific to her context. But it would be artificial and inappropriate for the Anglo-American to take over these same stories. She needs to draw on stories from her own cultural context.

## CLASSICAL AND INDUSTRIAL PATRIARCHIES

We have argued that all Christian feminists share a common heritage of religious arguments for women's marginalization and recent struggles against that heritage, although that common heritage has different nuances in different Christian cultural contexts. In addition Jewish and Christian feminists share some common traditions of sexism, but each tradition has distinct problems. For example Christians who dropped the rite of circumcision do not have to deal with a solely male ritual of incorporation into the communal covenant. Jewish feminists, who have no existing priesthood, do not have to deal with arguments against women in the priesthood.

But the potential for both conflict and solidarity among women in different cultures, classes, and races has another source beyond shared religious culture. All women today have experienced a global system of marginalization of women called patriarchy. Patriarchy has common characteristics cross-culturally, although it also takes distinct forms in different cultures, different socioeconomic systems, and at different class levels. Conflict among women is possible when the effects of class and racial status on the experience of patriarchy are not recognized. Solidarity among women is enhanced to the extent that they recognize these different experiences of patriarchy as variants within a larger system of patriarchal hierarchy that encompasses class and race hierarchy.

Patriarchy originated within a familial slave system of production. It has adapted in recent centuries to the dissolution of the familial slave system of production and its replacement by the capitalist system of production. It is important to recognize this shifting pattern of patriarchy with changing systems of production.

Some cultures, particularly in Asia, Africa, and among Native Americans, have preserved elements of Motherright that preceded the development of the full-blown patriarchal system. Cross-cultural dialogue on feminist issues needs to study elements of Motherright in non-Western cultures. This is not to be confused with matriarchy, which probably never existed. Motherright means that women as a group have spheres of control over property, production, and culture independent of men. But this does not mean that women are dominant. In most of these cultures men still predominate. Some traces of Motherright are also preserved in Hebrew Scripture and in early European societies. Patriarchy gradually suppressed these remnants of Motherright in Western culture.

The general characteristics of preindustrial patriarchal society are the following. Women in such societies are denied civil or legal rights in their own name. They cannot vote, represent themselves in law, make contracts, or in other ways be recognized as autonomous adults with legal standing. They have the permanent legal standing of children or dependents and are defined as the quasi-property of their fathers and later their husbands or other male relatives who are the "head of the household" where they reside. They can be physically punished, sometimes even killed, and sometimes sold or bought by males. They also have restricted rights to own or inherit property. They may be able to hold a dowry as a security against divorce or widowhood, but most of the property and titles in a family pass from father to son. The property of a woman is held or managed by her husband or other male relatives. Her children belong to her husband. Men can divorce women, but women cannot divorce men. At marriage a woman loses membership in her family and becomes a member of her husband's family. Her identity is seen as legally merged into that of her husband's family. Her husband represents her and exercises headship over her.

Such patriarchal societies also deny women higher education. The public offices of war, politics, and culture are seen as belonging exclusively to men. Women are denied access to the universities and other institutions that prepare men for professions and leadership in the public order. Religion reinforces this subordination of women in its symbolic systems and ecclesiastical codes and excludes women from theological education and official religious leadership. The woman, then, is restricted to the home. There she plays a double role as a wife and mother who bears and nurtures children, and as a worker in the domestic economy.

In preindustrial society this domestic economy was very extensive, since most of the goods of society were produced in the home or in workshops and farms attached to the home. Thus the woman played an extensive role as an economic worker (or as manager of domestic work) but lacked legal ownership of the fruits of her own labor. Her work belonged to her husband. Of course, exceptions to this system can be found in the cases of individual women, and women find means of secondary power and influence within it through their roles and relationships. But here this will have to suffice to describe the main outlines of women's status in classical patriarchy.

The fundamental change that takes place in capitalist industrialism is the loss of the economic role of the family or the domestic economy to a collectivized and industrialized form of production outside the home and no longer owned by the workers as family units. Women thus lose more and more of their productive economic role in the home. Instead the woman's role in the family is converted into being the manager of consumption, the nurturer in an intensified and prolonged system of child care (i.e., children remain economically dependent longer), and the housekeeper. Housekeeping now includes much more rigorous standards of cleanliness. With the loss of domestic servants, this role is taken over by the wife. The family shrinks from the extended to the nuclear family, so the adult woman is left as the only adult in the household in the absence of the husband who works outside the home.

A new ideology of the feminine arises to idealize this extended and intensified role of the wife and mother as nurturer, who is mandated to provide a compensatory sphere of rest and recuperation for the working males, as well as take care of their physical needs and raise the children. Industrialization creates a new rigid separation of spheres that separates male from female, work from home, the secular world of public work, war, and politics from the domestic realm of compensatory nurture. Religion is disestablished, privatized, and identified with the woman's sphere of the home. Religion comes to be seen as "feminine" rather than "masculine" as it was in classical patriarchy.

Poor women or working-class women are incorporated into the new industrial economy at doubly exploitative wages. This was true of children as well, although reform movements endeavored to remove child labor. Working women seldom do the same work as men but are drawn into special women's sectors of the industrial economy, where they work equally long hours but typically at 50 percent or less of comparable male wages. They are used as a marginal and superexploited sector of the labor force. Such working women are still expected to play the roles of wife, mother, and housekeeper in relation to husband and children, as the nonworking middle-class housewife. The non-working (i.e., doing only unpaid domestic work) housewife sets the official standards of "femininity" for the culture. The working-class woman is called to aspire to these same standards, although the society makes it impossible for her actually to do so. She is therefore regarded as not really a "lady"; that is, her womanhood is denied respect, which is given to the women of the ruling class who conform to the standards of normative "femininity."

As the industrial economy develops, more and more middle-class and married women are drawn into the labor force. Liberal reform movements ameliorate some of the bad conditions and poor wages of the workers, although their primary answer to the problem of the exploitation of women is to remove them from the labor force by providing a wage large enough for only the male head of the house to have to work. Liberal reformers also dissolve many of the structures of traditional patriarchal law that denied women civil rights, property rights, and access to higher education and professions. This reform of traditional patriarchal legal systems is brought about particularly by the women's movement within liberalism and generally is seen as culminating in granting women the vote. Women are officially recognized as legal persons in their own right.

## CONFLICT AND SOLIDARITY AMONG WOMEN

But this reform of women's position, legally and educationally, masks the new system of economic oppression of women that is being forged by industrialism. This system of patriarchy in liberal capitalism has several characteristics. First, all working women at whatever class level are expected to work a double shift. That is to say, paid labor is defined in terms of a male work day based on a wife who provides the domestic support structure for paid work. Working women must work the same work day as the male (part-time work being so marginal and poorly paid as not to be a viable option for most women). But they also are expected to do the same domestic work in child care, in house-keeping, and in providing the domestic support structure for the work-ers in the family as the normative "wife." Even in advanced industrial countries this work sector is about twenty-five to forty hours a week.

This double load fragments and defeats women's competence in both areas. On the one hand, she is blamed for being an inadequate wife and mother. All sorts of social evils are attributed to the fact that she works outside the home, although this work is essential for women who are single heads of households and increasingly necessary for couples as well. Second, her domestic work role structures her out of the more demanding professions that require extensive education, high mobility, extended hours away from the family, and so on. Thus women are kept at the bottom of their various professions.

Women who work are structured primarily into gender-segregated sectors of the economy that have low status, poor working conditions, low pay, and few fringe benefits. Women's work is seldom unionized. In the United States about 90 percent of the women who work do so in economic sectors that are entirely or predominantly female. This work at whatever level is thought of as auxiliary and inferior to the male labor to which it is related (for example, secretary to boss, nurse to doctor, waitress to owner or even head waiter). The cultural stereo-type of women's auxiliary and inferior relation to men is thus preserved in the paid labor structure, as well as the relation of women to men in the home.

Only a tiny percentage of women (about 3–5 percent in Western countries) work in those professions regarded as of high status and pay, such as lawyers, university professors, doctors. Even these women are found in the lower-paid sectors of these professions. Thus it is somewhat misleading to speak of middle-class women or ruling-class women as though they were comparable to middle-class or ruling-class men. Women, in fact, do not possess class status in the same way as men. Most women belong to particular classes because of their dependence on males of these classes as parents or husbands. Very few women could maintain upper-class status through their own means, with an independent income, apart from this dependency. This means that many women become impoverished when they are widowed or divorced. It has been shown that the fastest-growing sector in American society is female heads of households, whether of white or minority races. Such female-headed households account for the majority of families living in poverty.

One of the defects of the feminist movements in the Western middle-class context is that they have concentrated on promoting the equal pay and equal opportunities of women within this small sector of women working or aspiring to work in high-status, male-dominated professions. This orientation of middle-class white feminism obscures the total economic and cultural structure of sexist oppression. Black and third world women thus justifiably conclude that the feminist movement has nothing to do with them. The sort of feminist movement that is compatible with a liberation theology perspective must explicate the total system of women's oppression, looking at this question from the perspective of working-class and third world women. It must also examine the variants on industrialism that have emerged in the socialist systems.

It has often been said that women of the working class and third world suffer from "double oppression," oppression as women and as members of oppressed classes and racial groups. But the meaning of this phrase has not been fully explicated. "Double oppression" does not mean simply one kind of oppression as women and another kind as members of oppressed groups but, in addition, doubled kinds of *sexist* oppression that come from this multilayered oppression experienced by women of oppressed groups. One can analyze this compounding of sexist oppression on various areas.

On the level of their sexuality and sexual roles, women of the oppressed suffer double sexist oppression. First, they suffer the traditional kinds of oppression through their sexual roles in relation to the men of their own class or race (family). Their impoverished condition intensifies these problems; that is, birth control may not be available to them, the frustration experienced by men of their community may cause these men to take out their anger on women through sexual violence and wife battering, and so on. Second, they experience a denigration of their womanhood at the hands of men (and women) of the dominant classes and race. They may be expected to be sexually available to dominant males in the places where they work, and they are punished if they do not comply. As poor and minority women they are not granted the respect reserved for "ladies" of the dominant class and are humiliated by their inability to achieve the standards of the dominant "feminine" image and role.

On the economic level, poor women carry the double work roles of both the homemaker-mother and the paid worker. But they carry these double work roles under the most unfavorable conditions. They work in the most exploited sectors of the labor force reserved for minority and poor women. They suffer the lowest pay, the poorest working conditions. This poor pay, in turn, makes it even more difficult for them to carry their domestic role. They cannot pay for adequate food and shelter, much less for child care. Their children are often left alone at home or in the street without adequate supervision. They cannot be sure whether their children will still be alive or well and the house intact when they return. Their workplace may be far from where they live, and they must take long bus rides or walk long distances to their work. Thus the double work load is exacerbated in myriad ways for the woman of the poor.

At the level of culture, minority and third world women also suffer a double oppression. This is a particularly complicated area. It is important to consider the effects of Christianization and Westernization on women of the third world. For example, a particular African culture might have had practices of polygamy but also of women's associations through which women marketed their own produce and had economic independence. Christianization and Westernization seek to abolish polygamy, regarding such a practice as immoral. Western Christians may do so believing that they are actually elevating the status of women. Liberal reforms dissolve some of the traditional disabilities experienced by native women and bring the vote and university education to women. But such reforms are available primarily to a small elite of upper-class native women.

Meanwhile the poorer women experience the disruption of a traditional system of marriage without any adequate substitute; thus many former wives are left destitute. Also Western agricultural and industrial aid gives the tools of modernization to men under the Western capitalist assumption that men are the productive class. So women are deprived of the areas of economic power they once enjoyed. Third world women of the poor thus are caught between two patriarchal systems and often suffer the worst of both worlds, losing the traditional areas of power they once enjoyed and being unable to aspire to the new "rights for women" brought in for the upper classes.

Moreover men of their own country, who lead and define the agenda of the anticolonial liberation movement, may see themselves as throwing off the effects of Westernization and liberalization in such a way as to rescind some of the new rights won for women through this influence. They call for women to return to their traditional subordination in the name of affirming the traditional culture. Women are enjoined to step back and put on the veil or other such customs of women's subordination in the name of patriotism and commitment to the liberation struggle. This is why it is essential that the women's agenda be included in the liberation agenda and also that third world women be the primary spokespersons for the women's agenda.

It would be very important to contextualize this issue of double oppression in various specific cultural and historical contexts. What this means in certain cultures in Africa might be quite different from what it means in certain contexts in Asia or Latin America. This would be an important area for development of dialogue between third and first world women. One has only begun to glimpse the complex patterns set up for women by the double structures of oppression created by the superimposition of Christianity and Western industrialization on top of traditional cultures within the context of colonial dependency. What is needed is real dialogue across class, race, and cultural lines to explicate more fully the actual meaning of the double oppression of women within the systems of class, racial, and international economic oppression.

We have talked about both religious intercultural dialogue and a social dialogue that seeks to analyze the distinct contexts of women's oppression within patriarchy. What is the goal of this dialogue? Is the intention to create a universal culture? a universal religion? In what ways do our loyalties to our particular religious and ethnic communities put us in conflict with a concern for women and men outside these boundaries? I believe that our goals must be those of a just global socioeconomic and political system. Creating a just global order also demands a critique of ideologies, religious or secular. We must shape a culture that promotes mutuality rather than domination.

I believe this means that our first loyalty must be to the good of the human community as a whole in life-sustaining relationship to the earth or the biosphere. We must put aside parochial loyalties, whether of religion or ethnicity. We must be clear that any authentic God-Goddess must be the creator and sustainer of all life, available to all sentient beings, not simply an ethnocentric, androcentric, or anthropocentric deity. Humanity must grow up religiously from naive group-egoism to a concern for the welfare of the whole planetary community as the only context in which any of us can place our final loyalty.

This planetary loyalty is not incompatible with particular commitments to historical religious, ethnic, and regional communities. But this loyalty must be construed more in the sense of taking responsibility for our particular communities as the context in which we must act responsibly on behalf of the whole. We are working toward a planetary conversion of the model of power that has prevailed in human history at least since the rise of patriarchy some six thousand years ago. The model of power as dominance, reducing other humans and nonhumans to servitude, misery, and death, now threatens all of our collective life.

This pattern must be transformed to a model of power based on mutuality and biophilic values. Without losing all of the distinctiveness of our particular historical memories and cultural heritages, each culture must be transformed to enhance those trends that are biophilic and to overcome the trends that are necrophilic. Each religious culture must rise and converge on this common project of enhancing the loving and life-giving capacities of the human spirit in right relation to other beings. This is finally what redemption, or being in right relation to God-Goddess, is all about.

# 4

# Hispanic Theology in North America

## Orlando E. Costas

The context, method, and program of Hispanic theology in North America is a new type of liberation theology in the Americas. To be sure, as a formal discourse, Hispanic theology is still in an embryonic stage. What will be described, then, is an incipient discourse reflected in several anthologies, articles, academic courses, and monographs. These resources, nevertheless, are in themselves expressions of a living theology in the life, worship, and mission of Hispanic Christians in the United States and Puerto Rico. Puerto Rico, a colonial territory (culturally, geographically, and historically part of Latin America and the Caribbean), is politically integrated into the United States. At least one third of the Puerto Rican population lives in the continental United States, and there is a continuous flow between the island and the U.S. mainland. Thus it is not possible to leave Puerto Rico out of the universe of North American theology. It is the reality of an active community of faith critically attentive to the Word of God, seeking to obey God's will in a strange land, that ultimately verifies the existence of a Hispanic theological discourse.

Several factors explain why Hispanic theology has been so late in developing. The fact that Hispanics have had to live and work in the shadow of Latin American theology, on the one hand, and North American theologies (black, feminist, white male, and others), on the other, is not without significance. There is also a sense in which Hispanic-Americans have been deprived of a vernacular language. If to do theology is to reflect critically on the faith and to articulate coherently and contextually its meaning in the language of a particular community, Hispanic Christians have been denied the opportunity to do so by their lack of a proper grasp of either Spanish or English. After many years a handful of Hispanic theologians has acquired the courage and energy to begin to reflect out loud, in broken English and tarnished Spanish, on the faith in light of sociocultural reality.

## THE CONTEXT OF HISPANIC THEOLOGY

The context of Hispanic theology has been shaped by the experience of conquest, colonialism, migration, and biculturalism. The historical consciousness of conquest is mediated especially by the two leading Hispanic communities in North America—the Mexican and the Puerto Rican. The reality of colonialism has been experienced, especially, in the Southwest and Puerto Rico.

The Treaty of Guadalupe-Hidalgo (1848) was but the formalization of a progressive conquest by the United States of half the territory of Mexico, into which many U.S. citizens had been welcomed and others had penetrated illegally. Ironically, the descendants of the country that opened its doors to Anglos and lost a significant portion of its territory are designated today by United States immigration authorities as illegal aliens. The Treaty of Guadalupe-Hidalgo may have created a political border, but it could not impose a cultural one. Mexican families live today on both sides of the Rio Bravo. They have a historical and cultural claim to the Southwest. This region belongs as much to them as it does to Anglo-Americans. In the case of Puerto Rico, we have an occupied island, by whatever name: a federal territory, a commonwealth, a "free-associated state," or any other euphemism. The fact remains that Puerto Rico became part of the United States as war booty from the Spanish-American War (1898). This makes it plainly and simply a colony. Puerto Rican people have not had a chance to decide their own future, notwithstanding the so-called plebiscite of 1952. A colonized people cannot decide their political future if they are living under colonial rule.

This colonial reality extends to the Caribbean and Central America. Even though these regions are made up of supposedly independent nations, they are really neocolonies because of the regional domination of the United States. Thus, for example, Honduras had to give up its territorial integrity to accommodate several thousand U.S. troops stationed near the Nicaraguan border. Nicaragua was subjected to a counterrevolutionary war with the direct military support of the United

States, even as the Somocista dynasty was kept in power by the economic, political, and military support of the U.S. government. Costa Rica is being forced to give up the most precious value of its people (their peaceful character, and nonaligned tradition) in order "to play" its U.S. assignment. El Salvador is involved in a revolutionary war but without the possibility of a military victory in the foreseeable future for either the U.S.-backed government army or the national liberation front. Grenada was invaded by the United States in a flagrant violation of the Organization of American States charter. Guatemala, in spite of its recent democratic elections, is living the agony of suffering and death on account of political and economic corruption and a state of institutionalized repressive and subversive armed violence. Similar statements can be made about the Dominican Republic, Cuba, and several South American nations.

The painful experience of migration—external and internal—has further shaped the context of Hispanic theology. With the exception of the descendants of the early settlers of St. Augustine and Tampa (Florida), and the Southwest, Hispanics are either immigrants or their offspring. They bear in their collective memories the pain of becoming uprooted from their loved ones and cultures, adapting to a new environment, and struggling through social and economic hardship. They have come as political refugees, as immigrants in search of a better way of life, or as migrant workers. Most recently the Hispanic community has experienced a tremendous influx from Mexico, from Central America and the Caribbean, and to a lesser extent, from South America. The new immigrants have taken up jobs few seem to want in factories, farms, and restaurants. Not being able to get adequate documentation, they have been at the mercy of the Immigration and Naturalization Service and of their employers. Indeed they have become a new army of cheap labor, without benefits or rights, unable to anticipate what tomorrow might bring, subject to arrest and deportation at any moment. They cannot trust anybody—not even other (documented residents or U.S. born) Hispanics. The system has been so excruciating toward the new immigrants that it has created a split in the Hispanic community. Thus the experience of migration has not only been the result of an economic and political situation back home, in which the United States has not been a passive observer, but it has also been the result of a divisive factor (cultural and political) in the Hispanic community itself.

Another piece in the Hispanic contextual mosaic is the phenomenon of biculturalism. Hispanic Americans are the offspring of a double process of *mestizaje* (from *mestizo*, "hybrid," a racial and cultural mixture). The process has encompassed the triple encounter between European (Iberian), Amerindian, and African peoples, which is the direct result of the Spanish/Portuguese conquest and civilization that gave birth to the Latin American peoples. It has also involved the encounter between the Anglo-American civilization and the Latin American, which since 1848 has been giving way to a new Hispanic American community. This double mestizaje is the result of the military, cultural, and religious invasions and conquests that have characterized the history of Hispanics in North America. Each has produced multiple variants. The first mestizaje produced the multiple national and regional cultures of the Latin American mosaic; the second created the emerging regional and subcultural varieties to be found in Hispanic communities through the United States. Consequently, Mexican American and Central American groups have the imprint of the Spanish-Indian confrontation out of which emerged the Mexican and Mesoamerican peoples, whereas Puerto Ricans and other Hispanics from the eastern Caribbean reflect the Spanish-Amerindian-African confrontation.

Hispanic Americans belong to two worlds, and yet they are not bona fide members of either. They must communicate in two languages without having full ownership of either one. Virgilio Elizondo's description of a *mestizo* group, which he applies just to the Mexican American, is, nevertheless, a description of all Hispanics.

> A *mestizo* group represents a particularly serious threat to its two parent cultures. The *mestizo* does not fit conveniently into the analysis categories used by either parent group. The *mestizo* may understand them far better than they understand him or her. To be an insider-outsider, as is the *mestizo*, is to have closeness to and distance from both parent cultures. A mestizo people can see and appreciate the characteristics in its parent cultures that they see neither in themselves nor in each other. It is threatening to be in the presence of someone who knows us better than we know ourselves. (Elizondo 1983, 18)

Given this reality, Hispanic Americans have to struggle against the temptation of assimilation or isolation in order not to be a threat to their parent cultures. Either alternative will be detrimental to their collective future and their prophetic role in the Americas, which ultimately lies in the recovery of their bicultural identity. The future of Hispanics in the Americas lies neither in assimilation nor isolation but rather in the recovery and affirmation of their double identity.

## THE METHOD OF HISPANIC THEOLOGY

This explains why Hispanic theology has used what might be described as a historicocultural method. Three steps may be identified as characterizing this approach.

The first is to *remember* the rich cultural heritage of the Hispanic peoples in the Americas and the events that have led the various Hispanic groups in North America to their present situation. This pilgrimage backward is necessary in order to move forward. Without a recovery of their historical and cultural roots, Hispanics will not be able to transcend their alienated consciousness introjected by the dominant sectors of North American society through many years of conquest and domination. Indeed, the pilgrimage to the past is essential not only to overcome all the stereotype images and inferior status Hispanics have been led to believe about themselves but especially to recover the liberating potential of their religiocultural heritage. Whether Catholic or Protestant the Hispanic religious past is filled with powerful symbols of resistance, survival, and hope. Unfortunately, the social and theological significance of these symbols has been blurred, distorted, or minimized by non-Hispanic interpreters. One of the first tasks of a liberating Hispanic theology is to read anew, from within, and restore the "subversive" and "liberating" memory of Hispanics in North America.

The second step is to *correlate* the past with the present. We must examine the Hispanic reality in North America and the Caribbean—and indeed in the entire third world. We must correlate the experience of "outsiders" (Hispanics) with the reality of "insiders" (North Americans). Finally, we must correlate the personal and social existence of Hispanics with the triune God whose Eternal Word has been revealed in Jesus, whose Spirit is present in the struggles of Hispanic history and culture, and who has been sent to set the world free, to reconcile it with God and thus bring glory to the one who was, who is, and who will always be.

1. To correlate "now and then" is to explore the historical linkage between the present reality of Hispanics and the cultural and religious tradition. Hispanic Protestants must come to terms with their Catholic cultural background. Indeed they must confront the fact that Anglo-Saxon Protestantism has, by and large, denied them theological access to their cultural heritage and values. Catholics must be aware of the *chiroscuro* (obscure) past of Iberian-Catholic Christianity in the Americas—its oppressive and alienating role. Moreover, as Hispanic Catholics

in North America they must confront the fact that European Catholic theology and practice have been repressive forces against the Hispanic-American Catholic church. Hispanic liberation theology passes through a process of emancipation from other cultural traditions *within* the North American church.

2. The correlation of "here and there" involves a comparative reflection between the situation in Latin America and the United States. Since being Hispanic implies being linked historically and culturally with the Iberian-American world, it is not possible to be and act as an Hispanic-American without understanding the Latin American cultural experience and social reality. Being a Neorican (U.S.–born Puerto Rican) is, to be sure, different from being a Puerto Rican islander. But it is not possible to claim a Puerto Rican identity without understanding what the island is culturally all about and appreciating its contemporary struggles. (Likewise, it is not possible for Puerto Rican islanders to claim a twentieth-century patriotic identity without understanding the Puerto Rican diaspora in the U.S. mainland.) By the same token, being a Chicano (U.S.–born Mexican) is different from being a Mexican. But it is not possible to be a true Chicano without coming to terms with Mexico, just as a twentieth-century Mexican identity must deal with the *larger* Mexican reality, including the two-hundred-plus aboriginal groups spread throughout the republic and the millions *al norte* (to the north) in Mexican-related groups throughout the United States.

3. The correlation of the experience of "outsiders" with "insiders" involves a confrontation with the reality of a minority community in a dominant society. This minority community is aware of its alien status and yet is free to be itself and contribute to the well-being of all. This implies a fundamental challenge to the notion of Anglo-white supremacy expressed historically in the ideologies of "manifest destiny" and "the melting pot." Over against the traditional Anglo view that one can maintain one's ethnicity and speak other languages besides English so long as it is not done publicly, Hispanic theology insists on the *public* value of a culturally heterogeneous society, the proven social benefits of a bilingual society, and the cultural impoverishment of monolingualism. Furthermore, Hispanic theology demands a space in North American culture and society not only to learn and teach the language and traditions of the Hispanic peoples and reflect on the faith from within its historicocultural heritage but also to make a sociotheological contribution to North American society. To do so is to demand that Hispanics be taken seriously and not be simply tokens used for political

gains every four years or as an attractive new market to be exploited with promotional gimmicks. Though Hispanics stand "outside the gate" of mainstream North American society, Hispanic theology enables them to stand tall and be seen! Though they speak with a "broken accent," they are empowered to speak the truth loud and clear and make their cry for justice heard in the centers of power.

4. The correlation of the personal and social existence of Hispanics with the revelation of the triune God enables Hispanic theology to plumb the depths of faith implicit in the Hispanic experience. Indeed it is not possible to understand the Hispanic struggle for liberation apart from the faith of a people in what is described in the Afro-Brazilian *Quilombo's Mass* as

> . . . the God of all names . . .
> who makes all people of
> tenderness and . . . dust . . .
> the Father, who makes
> all flesh, the Black and
> the white, red in the blood.
> . . . the Son, Jesus our brother,
> who was born dark of the
> race of Abraham.
> . . . the Holy Spirit, banner
> and song . . .
> the true God who loved us first
> Without divisions
> . . . The Three who are one
> only God. (Nascimento)

God has never been a stranger for the Hispanic community, since God was known to their forebears. For Hispanics are a Spirit-conscious people deeply aware of the presence of the almighty in their history. This awareness, however, is not so much rooted in reason or nature as in the story of Jesus. It is through Christ that Hispanics have made the link between Yahweh and the supreme deity of their forebears. The Spirit that binds the Hispanic tradition is none other than the Spirit of Christ. Thus Christology lies at the center of Hispanic theology. To explore the relationship between Hispanic reality and faith, it is necessary in the first place to ask, Who is Jesus Christ for Hispanics? This is vividly demonstrated in a "Canon of Puerto Rican Nostalgia" by Antonio M. Stevens-Arroyo (1980, 113–14):

. . . when our [forebears] sinned
and lost the beauty of Eden,
you did not abandon us,
but promised a new Adam (Gen. 3:15; Rom. 5:12ff.).
Christ your only Son.

Rich as he was, he made himself poor for our
sake
in order to make us rich
by means of his poverty. . . .

In the fullness of time,
with a happiness beyond reason. . . .
Christ the savior set out from the mountains
of
Galilee
Travelling by the footpaths of the
countryside,
he brought the tidings of good news to the
City
of [humanity].
Scorned for his humble birth (Isa. 53:2ff.;
Matt. 26:73; John [1:]46),
slighted for his parables and manner of
speech,
he was rejected by this world's wisdom
as a *jíbaro*[1] in a city of heartlessness.

But he bore his sufferings without violence,
offering his life as a ransom for many. . . .

Remember the faithful
who walked through the valley of darkness on
their
way to you;
those who earned their bread by the sweat of
their
brows,
those who toiled in the heat of the tropical
sun
and who fell in their youth like cane under
the
*machete.*[2]
And do not forget those who offered their
life's
blood

in patient pursuit of a freedom
which still remains your promise to us. . . .

But we recall that you summoned Abraham from
his
homeland,
that you led Moses in the Exodus,
and John the Baptist in the desert.
As Christ hung on the cross between earth and
sky,
we are crucified in a Limbo,
belonging neither here nor there
because you have given us the lot of serving
you
as a solitary spirit in great expectation. . . .

O that our plea would be your praise!
Because we do not see the *flamboyán*[3]
in this gray jungle of steel and cement,
we seek you with a faith more pure,
because we do not hear the song of the
*coquí*[4]
above the din of people in the streets,
we bless you with proven faithfulness.
Because we do not dance in the *barrio*[5] or
*batey*[6]
we paint a mechanized world
the color of an eternal smile.

Exiles twice-over from the Promised Land,
we speak to you with the stubborn badgering,
*la*
*peleíta monga*,[7] of a child
until we can glorify you with
straightforwardness.

*Ay Bendito*,[8] Lord!
We will never be able to praise you as you
deserve.
But if our prayer is united with Christ's,
we will have a song for thanking you.

Through him,
with him, in him,
Almighty Father,
in the unity of the Holy Spirit,
all glory and honor is yours,
forever and ever. Amen.

In this prayer we see the connection between Christ and the Hispanic community. He is viewed as the promised Son of God who became a Galilean *jíbaro* and lived the Hispanic experience of poverty, ignorance, being "slighted . . . manner of speech," rejection, loneliness, exile, suffering, and death to lead them "to the Almighty . . . in the unity of the Holy Spirit."

The correlation between reality and faith is thus achieved christologically. Yet, as the prayer demonstrates, Christology opens the way for a much larger connecting link (between God and humanity) and a more concrete expression of faith (the Hispanic church).

The third and concluding step in Hispanic theology is the *articulation* of the insights derived from the process of correlation in a coherent discourse. Inevitably, this involves a theological account of the spiritual journey of the Hispanic community as lived and expressed in the various Hispanic churches. It implies a new and more Hispanically oriented reading of the Scriptures and Christian history. It assumes a Hispanic interpretation of traditional Christian doctrines. Above all, it presupposes the formulation of a new missiology inspired in the festive spirit of the Hispanic community, informed by the joyous character of the gospel, and focused on the God who wills life for the whole earth.

## THE PROGRAM OF HISPANIC THEOLOGY

The program of Hispanic theology is still in the process of design. Even so, we can identify at least a three-point agenda.

The first and most immediate item in the Hispanic theological agenda is to explore the depth of the faith and praxis of the Hispanic church in light of God's Word, Hispanic tradition, and the Hispanic experience in North America. Hispanic theology seeks to plumb the faith that the various Hispanic Christian communities celebrate, live, and confess. These communities spread across denominational, social, and subcultural boundaries. They have an admittedly varied but still common bond to the Christian Scriptures. They are linked to the Christian tradition as it has been handed down in sundry ways to their various groups. Most of all, they share the experience of living their faith as pilgrims in a strange land. Hispanic theology works with these sources as it reflects on the faith of the Hispanic church, articulating its meaning in an ordered and coherent manner. Thus the first task of Hispanic theology is to help the Hispanic Christian community understand and appreciate the faith it professes and lives.

But theology is not only a discipline that orders and clarifies the faith; it also reflects critically on its practice. The second task of Hispanic theology, therefore, is to enable the Hispanic church to become theologically critical of its life and mission. This is done by critically reflecting on the praxis of Hispanic Christians amid the historical challenges facing the Hispanic community. The aim here is not simply to help the church be ethically consistent with the faith it professes but especially to set it free for service in the Hispanic community. In so doing, Hispanic theology seeks to contribute to the emergence of a historically committed church, critically and prayerfully engaged in the struggle for a more humane, free, just, and peaceful society with women and men in the United States and the Americas.

The third point in the Hispanic theological agenda is engagement in a constructive critical dialogue with other theologies in the Americas. As a theology of an oppressed group, it is open for dialogue with the theological reflections of other oppressed communities. Hispanic theology has already received much inspiration and many insights from Latin American and black theologies. It shares with them a common journey. Like both of them, Hispanic theology has much to learn from feminist theology. Each of these theologies poses questions of class, race, and sex that touch upon the Hispanic reality in North America. Indeed Hispanic theology may yet bring forth the racist-classist-sexist-reality behind oppressive structures in the Americas, demonstrating its potential to learn from its much older and sophisticated partners. By the same token, it challenges all of them to see the cultural-linguistic dimensions of oppression, the complementary nature of their respective discourses, and the need to move beyond one-sided social analyses and theological formulations. The struggle for liberation is far more complex than what any perspective can encompass. For the same reason, Hispanics will also have to remain open to the contributions and critiques of other liberation theologies in the Americas. Such an openness and constructive dialogue will help Hispanic theology promote solidarity for joint action toward global justice and peace.

## References

Elizondo, Virgilio. 1983. *Galilean Journey: The Mexican-American Promise*. Maryknoll: Orbis Books.

Nascimento, Milton, Pedro Casaldaliga, Pedro Tierra, and Helder Camara. *Quilombo's Mass*. Trans. from the Portuguese by Ruy Costa.

Stevens-Arroyo, Antonio, ed. 1980. *Prophets Denied Honor: An Anthology of the Hispanic Church in the United States.* Maryknoll: Orbis Books.

# Notes

1. *Jíbaro:* "the Puerto Rican peasant or mountan [person]" (Stevens-Arroyo 1980, 114).

2. *Machete:* "a large knife used to cut sugar cane."

3. *Flamboyán:* "the flame tree, noted for its bright red-orange flowers; it is very common in Puerto Rico."

4. *Coquí:* "small frog, native to Puerto Rico, noted for its high-pitched call."

5. *Barrio:* "an outlying district."

6. *Batey:* "an Indian word for the unpaved central plaza of the village: it has come to mean the area immediately surrounding a house where people gather to talk or socialize."

7. *La peleíta monga:* "an idiomatic Puerto Rican expression for a way of 'beating around the bush' in order to gain something."

8. *Ay Bendito!:* "a traditional Puerto Rican exclamation that has been weighted with connotations of fatalism by contemporary commentators."

# 5

# Jewish Theology of Liberation: Critical Thought and Messianic Trust

## Marc H. Ellis

In a fascinating and important book, *Against the Apocalypse: Responses to Catastrophe in Modern Jewish Culture*, David Roskies examines the history of the Jewish people through its various responses to destruction. What Roskies finds is a people with a remarkable ability to reclaim ancient Jewish archetypes and thereby create meaning within suffering and death. "The greater the catastrophe, the more the Jews have recalled the ancient archetypes," Roskies writes (1984, 198). And so in the ghettos of eastern Europe the archetypes of destruction were alive in the minds of the common people and intellectual alike: "The burning of the Temple (the sacred center), the death of the martyr (the sacred person), and the pogrom (the destruction of the Holy community)" (198). The walls and barbed wire that separated the Jews from the non-Jewish population paradoxically helped to bring some of the internal boundaries down:

> The elite were brought closer to the masses, the assimilated closer to the committed, the secular closer to the religious, Yiddish closer to Hebrew. The modernists became, despite their long battles against it, part of the literature of consolation. With the ghetto's intellectuals moving closer to the people, the writers could use the polylingualism of Jewish eastern Europe to restore conceptually and socially the idea of a Jewish nation that was the

penultimate consolation for the ultimate destruction. And a literature that was for centuries retrospective (including "prophecies after the fact") became increasingly prophetic—so that, in fact, analogies could be used at last not for consolation but for action, including uprisings. (197–98)

The scribes of the ghetto wrote as an act of faith and, in fact, participated in and transformed the "liturgy of destruction" that the Jewish people had articulated over the millennia. Though overwhelmingly secular in background and outlook, the ghetto writings continually referred to religious themes. Yitzhak Katzenelson, a secular poet, organized a public reading of the Bible on the day the Warsaw Ghetto was sealed, though this was to demonstrate a continuity of history as a people rather than belief in God. When it came to the Psalms, however, Katzenelson rejected them as too placid a form of response to catastrophe. At the same time Hillel Zeitlin, for years a modern religious existentialist, began translating the Psalms into Yiddish. When his ghetto tenement was blockaded Zeitlin arrived at the roundup point for deportation dressed in a prayer shawl and tefillin (Roskies 1984, 212).

We have here, in its most difficult articulation, memory as a form of resistance: the refusal to cut oneself from one's own people while at the same time speaking to the world in cries of anguish. Roskies concludes that to understand the collective response of the Jewish people one must look to the writers "who because they shared the same fate and were intimately involved in all facets of the people's Armageddon, were able to transmute the screams into a new and terrible scripture" (Roskies 1984, 202).

Today nearly fifty years after the Warsaw Ghetto uprising and its subsequent liquidation, these archetypes of destruction take on new form in a recently empowered Jewish people. It is not too much to say that the liturgy of destruction has come to legitimate that which it originally resisted: occupation and intervention, expropriation and statelessness, torture and murder. Memory as a form of resistance (the religious existentialist translating the Psalms and arriving for deportation with prayer shawl and tefillin) is replaced with memory as a form of oppression (scripture read to justify settlements in occupied territories and armed invasions in Lebanon). This "new and terrible scripture" continues to be written now with the blood of others (Ellis 1987, 45–46).

The liturgy of destruction, articulated in many ways, is known and felt by the Jewish people around the world and especially in the two most powerful Jewish communities, North America and Israel. But that part of the liturgy, the oppression of Palestinians as it has developed since the Six Day War in June 1967, is unspoken or denied. To speak of it is to face grave consequences, including the threat of excommunication and, still worse, the charge that one is creating the context for another holocaust. Yet honesty demands an accounting because the archetypes of the Temple, the martyr, and the pogrom are being played out in an arena where the persecuted are no longer powerless Jews but Palestinians and others who exist on the other side of Jewish Israeli power.

## HOLOCAUST THEOLOGY

The liturgy of destruction gave birth after World War II to a powerful and radical theology, Holocaust theology. Coming from the periphery of Jewish life, this theology challenged Jewish religious and secular perspectives by claiming the Holocaust as the formative event of contemporary Jewish life. To be a Jew is to stand within the event of Holocaust, to see this as the orienting event of our lives. The Holocaust calls for a renewed commitment to being Jewish even as it shatters the previous categories within which modern Jews live. The nineteenth-century categories of Orthodox and Reform Judaism with their understanding of Torah and the prophetic, as well as secular liberal and radical ideologies with their optimistic understanding of progress and universalism, must all be rethought in light of the Holocaust. Thus Holocaust theology challenges the entire religious and secular structure of Jewish life with its entrenched institutions, interests, and assumptions. That which stood at the center previous to the Holocaust—the synagogue, liberalism, radical politics—ultimately recedes to secondary positions. According to Holocaust theology the future of the Jewish people is found in remembrance and self-empowerment rather than prayer or politics (Ellis 1987, 7–24, 28–37).

Though Holocaust theologians are known and celebrated today— Elie Wiesel, Emil Fackenheim, and Richard Rubenstein, for example— their initial works were met as much with derision and conflict as enthusiasm and gratitude. The reasons for this reception involve the religious questions they raise as well as the new institutions they call for to pursue empowerment; both challenge Jewish leadership and sensibilities. To overcome these obstacles and create a norm for the Jewish community today, Holocaust theology simply speaks to the depths of Jewish historical experience and thus to the Jewish people.

---

Despite differing perspectives within Holocaust theology, its aspect of remembrance and empowerment assumes a religious significance. Holocaust theologians surface the dialectic of Holocaust and empowerment that is the command of the Holocaust victims to survive and flourish as a people in a hostile world. The major expression of this is found in the State of Israel and a politically active Jewish community in the United States. Yet that command is shadowed by the haunting cries of the ghetto scribes: The Holocaust event critiques all unjust use of power, even if that power is wielded by Jews. Though empowerment is mandated, the Holocaust calls for an ethic tried in the death camps of Auschwitz and Treblinka. The cry "Never Again" represents a demand to the world on behalf of the Jewish people as well as a hope that no people in the future shall suffer as the Jews have (Ellis 1987, 20–22).

From the beginning, this dialectic of Holocaust and empowerment was couched in symbolic language, and as the years passed political and military realities often superseded the radical, indeed prophetic, statements of earlier years. Holocaust theology meant something quite different before the 1967 Six Day War than after, before the 1973 Yom Kippur War than after, before the 1982 Lebanese War than after, before the 1987 uprising in the occupied territories than after. Critical to these changes is the increasingly militaristic and annexationist policies of Israel in the Middle East, the new global role of arms merchant and counter insurgency expert played by Israel, and the expanded role of the United States as Israel's guarantor and funding agency. In fact Holocaust theology did change to meet these changing historical realities by downplaying that side of the dialectic that critiqued unjust power and emphasizing the importance of empowerment in a hostile world. By the 1980s the Jewish community faced an intriguing and dangerous paradox: a radical theology that is politically neoconservative. Despite the protests and the public anguish expressed by some of the Holocaust theologians over certain Israeli and U.S. policies, it is fair to characterize the three best-known theologians—Wiesel, Fackenheim, and Rubenstein—and hosts of other intellectuals, theologians or not, as political neoconservatives. In this way they mirror a shift in the Jewish community at large even as they provide theological legitimation for this movement (Rubenstein 1975, 95–97).

Nowhere is this shift more evident than in the progressive theologian and activist Irving Greenberg. In an important and radical analysis of the Holocaust and its implications published in 1974, Greenberg wrote that after the Holocaust "no statement theological or otherwise can be made that is not credible in the presence of the burning children" and that the victims of the Holocaust ask us above all else "not to allow the creation of another matrix of values that might sustain another attempt at genocide." Greenberg affirmed empowerment as an essential aspect of fidelity to the victims of the Holocaust, although he added the proviso that to remember suffering propels the Jewish community to refuse to create other victims:

> The Holocaust cannot be used for triumphalism. Its moral challenge must also be applied to Jews. Those Jews who feel no guilt for the Holocaust are also tempted to moral apathy. Religious Jews who used the Holocaust to morally impugn every other religious group but their own are the ones who are tempted thereby into indifference at the Holocaust of others (cf. the general policy of the American Orthodox rabbinate on United States Vietnam policy). Those Israelis who place as much distance as possible between the weak, passive Diaspora victims and the "mighty Sabras" are tempted to use Israeli strength indiscriminately (i.e., beyond what is absolutely inescapable for self-defense and survival), which is to risk turning other people into victims of the Jews. Neither faith nor morality can function without serious twisting of perspective, even to the point of becoming demonic, unless they are illuminated by the fires of Auschwitz and Treblinka. (Greenberg 1977, 22, 27, 28, 29)

By the 1980s Greenberg's understanding of the Holocaust as critique was overshadowed by the difficult task of empowerment. He commented favorably on the reemergence of American power. He applauded Reagan's arms build-up, the stationing of medium-range missiles in Europe, the development of the Strategic Defense Initiative, the U.S. support for rebel forces in Angola, the withdrawal of the United States from UNESCO, and the funding of the Contras in Nicaragua. Greenberg's emphasis on empowerment allowed him to take the high road when analyzing Ronald Reagan's trip to Bitburg in May 1985:

> Overall Ronald Reagan's record in commemorating the Holocaust has been very good. He serves as honorary chairman of the campaign to create a national memorial. He has held commemorations of the Holocaust in the White House and spoken passionately of the need to remember. His support for Israel—the single most powerful Jewish commitment that the Holocaust shall not recur, the haven where most of the survivors built their new lives— is exemplary. Our criticism of this particular callous misjudgment must not be allowed to falsify the total overall picture, which is a good one. And we shall have to work with him again. (Greenberg 1985, 4)

In a revealing theological and political transformation, the ultimate danger has become the prophetic critique of empowerment.

When empowerment suffices in and of itself, religious language, already chastened by the event of mass death, takes on a form that Jews have rarely experienced in the last two thousand years. Empowerment becomes like a god. More specifically, and especially in the diaspora, the State of Israel assumes a deified existence. Of course, Israel-as-God has many ramifications, not the least of which is the diminution of critical thought. How can we understand the history that gave birth to Israel and the history it is now creating if we place Israel above history—as if it transcends critical analysis? Could we say that Holocaust theology, born amidst a harrowing and challenging epoch as a creative response to destruction, no longer provides the tools of analysis that enable us to understand the concrete history we as a people are creating? It should not surprise us that Holocaust theologians speak more often about Palestinian terrorism than about continuing Israel repression in the occupied territories, more often about the importance of Israel as a strategic ally of the United States than about Israel's support of repressive regimes in South Africa, Central America, and other regions around the globe.

## TOWARD A JEWISH THEOLOGY OF LIBERATION

Today we need a new Jewish theology that speaks of the horrors of the Holocaust and the need for empowerment yet seeks empowerment defined by an ethical path. It needs to articulate our situation as it is rather than as we hoped it would be. A new Jewish theology speaks of a renaissance of Jewish life as well as its cost: Israel as an occupying power, expropriator of land, torturer of prisoners, and arms exporter. The return to Israel may be our ideology; a new Jewish theology faces the fact that 75 percent of the Jewish people do not and will not live in Israel and that now more Israelis left Israel each year than emigrated to it. Even today, the vast Soviet immigration to Israel is forced rather than voluntary. The fastest growing diaspora community in the world today is made up of Israelis who leave Israel. A new Jewish theology must critically evaluate our success and power in North America and its consequences: single issue politics, uncritical support of U.S. foreign policy, alliance with economic classes and religious communities that are conservative and traditionally anti-Semitic. In short, a new Jewish theology begins by highlighting that which Holocaust theology has been unable to articulate—the cost of our empowerment (Ellis 1987, 25–46).

Difficult and dangerous as it might seem, by emphasizing the cost of empowerment the difference between empowerment and liberation comes into focus. A dialectical tension, once found in Holocaust theology, reemerges, and thus theology's critical edge can come to the fore. Empowerment is critiqued by its cost and is seen less as an end in itself. Instead it becomes a necessary and flawed step along the path toward a more comprehensive and fulfilling liberation. We have boldly proclaimed that the world cannot claim liberation without our own; so we face the reality that we are not liberated until all are, even those we may name as enemy.

A Jewish theology that broadens the contours of empowerment to liberation is born and named as a Jewish theology of liberation. It states unequivocally that solidarity with our own people and the ethical values that form the center of our tradition and solidarity with all peoples who are struggling for justice, including the Palestinian people, are at the center of the personal and communal life of the Jewish people. Solidarity, however, like empowerment, cannot remain on the level of principle or high-minded phraseology. Rather our concrete solidarity, or lack thereof, needs to be stated in detail, politically and religiously. For example, the continuing Israeli relationship with South Africa demonstrates a lack of solidarity with the struggle of the South African people and thus critiques our empowerment. A religiosity that makes biblical claims for the land for a people without a land and justifies the expulsion of those who have lived on the land is a critique of the religious foundations of our empowerment (Ellis 1987, 116).

Resources for such a theology of liberation are surfacing within the Jewish community today, though they are not without their own contradictions. Arthur Waskow's neoorthodox theology attempts to articulate a justice agenda, though he retains a safe distance from the critical question of Israel and proffers too heavy a dose of unreflective mysticism. Organizations like New Jewish Agenda bring together secular and religious Jews around a common ethical pursuit, but they remain on the fringe of the larger community. Movements in Israel like Oz veShalom (Religious Zionists for Strength and Peace) address the increasingly militaristic religious community but remain small in number and ineffectual. Jewish feminists continue to address the patriarchal qualities of Jewish organization, learning, and ritual in important ways, though a broader political agenda is in need of exploration. The new journal *Tikkun*, formed in response to the neoconservative journal *Commentary*, seeks to address the political and religious issues in a different key; whether it can escape a concern for legitimacy within the Jewish community leaves the outcome of this endeavor in doubt. Despite their various limitations, however, these remain prophetic attempts on the periphery of established Jewish power.

Yet the plain and bold language needed at this juncture of our history is missing. The critical issue of power and oppression—the breakthrough point—is talked around or submerged in slogans and ritual claims of loyalty to the community. The suffering continues, even escalates, at the same time that our theology and activity become more refined. We are in a state of paralysis as our affluence and power grow. Even the progressive movements within Jewish life remain in the dialectic of Holocaust and empowerment, unable to move toward liberation, for to enter the terrain of liberation is to call into question at a radical level the structures and perspectives of the Jewish community now built upon the foundations of Holocaust theology.

To say that, for the most part, these voices are missing within the Jewish community is a sad and lamentable fact; yet some Jewish voices do speak out in the language of liberation. For many who have spoken in the past, and many who speak today, are ostracized from the community and even in some cases excommunicated. They, like the ghetto scribes, are mostly secular, meticulously analyzing the history we are creating. Together they comprise a hidden tradition that calls the Jewish community to a difficult fidelity (Feuerlicht 1983, 280–81). In doing this they help lay the groundwork for a Jewish theology of liberation.

## RECOVERING THE HIDDEN TRADITION

The "hidden tradition" was first analyzed by Hannah Arendt, a German Jewish philosopher who emigrated to France after Hitler's rise to power in 1933 and then to the United States in 1941. Though her two greatest works, *The Origins of Totalitarianism* and *The Human Condition*, established her reputation as a political philosopher, her book *Eichmann in Jerusalem* is the best known to the general public because of the controversy it caused and the vehement condemnation she received by the Jewish press. The tone of criticism, often heard today, is best summed up by a letter the great Jewish scholar Gershom Scholem wrote Arendt in 1963: "In the Jewish tradition there is a concept, hard to define and yet concrete enough, which we know as *Ahabath Israel*: 'Love of the Jewish people. . . .' In you, dear Hannah, as in so many intellectuals who came from the German Left, I find little trace of this" (Arendt 1978, 241).

Yet it was Arendt's independence and critical thought that rankled the Jewish community rather than the substance of her philosophy. In fact it was her recovery and transformation of the hidden tradition of recent Jewish history that allowed her the space to think through the difficulties of our age and interweave the particular plight of the Jewish people with the broader contours of Western history. She was, in Russell Jacoby's terminology, a public intellectual, deeply Jewish though free of Jewish institutional pressure and power (Arendt 1978, 67–91).

According to Arendt, the hidden tradition began almost two hundred years ago with the Enlightenment and Jewish emancipation in Western Europe. This gave rise to greater participation of Jews in society, even as they remained outsiders in the social and political realms. This outcast status gave rise to two particular types of Jews in society: the "conscious pariahs," who transcended the bounds of nationality to "weave the strands of their Jewish genius into the general texture of European life," and the "parvenus," who tried to achieve status by raising themselves above their fellow Jews into the respectable world of the Gentiles. Arendt chose to place herself as a conscious pariah and thus endured a dual difficulty that all conscious pariahs shared, becoming marginal in relation to European society and to the Jewish community as well. As Ron Feldman analyzes the situation, conscious pariahs were "neither parochially Jewish, like their Eastern European cousins, nor were they part of the wealthy Jewish upper class of bankers and merchants that controlled Jewish-Gentile relations." The conscious pariah constituted a hidden tradition because there were few links between those who affirmed their pariah status—for example Heinrich Heine, Sholem Aleichem, Franz Kafka, and Walter Benjamin—or ties with the rest of the Jewish community. Standing exclusively neither inside nor outside their Jewish or European heritage, conscious pariahs used both as platforms from which to gain insight into the other (Feldman 1978, 18–19).

Amid the tumult of the twentieth century, with its reign of mass dislocation and mass death, particularly seen in the Jewish Holocaust, the pariah could no longer afford the role as simply outsider: The pariah had to become political. Thus Arendt recognized the creation of a Jewish homeland in Palestine as essential to the future of the Jewish people.

Arendt's Zionism, however, was from the beginning critical and non-statist. Though chastised and hidden from view today, Arendt's support for and warnings about the Zionist experiment are relevant in the present (Arendt 1978, 192).

Just months after the partition of Palestine and the establishment of a Jewish state in 1948, Arendt wrote a perceptive and troubling essay, "To Save the Jewish Homeland: There Is Still Time." According to Arendt the declaration of statehood had polarized positions on both sides: non-Zionist Jews were now diehard enthusiasts and moderate Palestinian Arabs were being forced to choose sides. Palestinian Jews and American Jews were essentially in agreement on the following propositions, propositions Arendt felt were detrimental to the possibility of peace:

> The moment had now come to get everything or nothing, victory or death; Arab and Jewish claims are irreconcilable and only a military decision can settle the issue; the Arabs—all Arabs—are now our enemies and we accept this fact; only outmoded liberals believe in compromises, only philistines believe in justice, and only schlemiels prefer truth and negotiation to propaganda and machine guns; Jewish experience in the last decades—or over the last centuries, or over the last two thousand years—has finally awakened us and taught us to look out for ourselves; this alone is reality, everything else is stupid sentimentality; everybody is against us, Great Britain is anti-Semitic, the United States is imperialist—but Russia might be our ally for a certain period because her interests happen to coincide with ours; yet in the final analysis we count upon nobody except ourselves; in sum—we are ready to go down fighting, and we will consider anybody who stands in our way a traitor and anything done to hinder us a stab in the back. (Arendt 1978, 181)

Arendt saw this unanimity of opinion as ominous, though characteristic of our modern mass age. It tended to dissuade discussion and reduce social relationships to those of an "ant heap": "A unanimous public opinion tends to eliminate bodily those who differ, for mass unanimity is not the result of agreement, but an expression of fanaticism and hysteria. In contrast to agreement, unanimity does not stop at certain well-defined objects, but spreads like an infection into every related issue." The loyal opposition, so important to critical thought and politics, was in the process of being eliminated. For Arendt the two great contributions of Jewish settlement, the Kibbutz movement and Hebrew University, as well as the great precedent of cooperation between a European and a colonized people were in danger of collapse. The advantage of the Jewish people in having no imperialist past to live down was also threatened, and thus their ability to act as a vanguard in international relations on a "small but valid scale" was being lost. Even if the Jews won the war and affirmed their claim to statehood, the unique possibilities and achievements of Zionism in Palestine would be destroyed:

> The land that would come into being would be something quite other than the dream of world Jewry, Zionist and non-Zionist. The "victorious" Jews would live surrounded by an entirely hostile Arab population, secluded inside ever-threatened borders, absorbed with physical self-defense to a degree that would submerge all other interests and activities. The growth of a Jewish culture would cease to be the concern of the whole people; social experiments would have to be discarded as impractical luxuries; political thought would center around military strategy; economic development would be determined exclusively by the needs of war. And all this would be the fate of a nation that—no matter how many immigrants it could still absorb and how far it extended its boundaries (the whole of Palestine and Transjordan is the insane Revisionist demand)—would still remain a very small people greatly outnumbered by hostile neighbors. (Arendt 1978, 187).

The ends of such an endeavor were clear to Arendt: degeneration into a warrior state with the political initiative in terrorist hands. The Jewish state could only be erected at the price of a Jewish homeland (Arendt 1978, 182, 184, 186, 188, 189).

Arendt closed her essay with the following proposition and hope:

1) The real goal of the Jews in Palestine is the building up of a Jewish homeland. This goal must never be sacrificed to the pseudosovereignty of a Jewish state.

2) The independence of Palestine can be achieved only on a solid basis of Jewish-Arab cooperation. As long as Jewish and Arab leaders both claim that there is "no bridge" between Jews and Arabs (as Moshe Shertok has just put it), the territory cannot be left to the political wisdom of its own inhabitants.

3) Elimination of all terrorist groups (and not agreements with them) and swift punishment of all terrorist deeds (and not merely protests against them) will be the only valid proof that the Jewish people in Palestine has recovered its sense of political reality and that Zionist leadership is again responsible enough to be trusted with the destinies of the Yishuv.

4) Immigration to Palestine, limited in numbers and in time, is the only "irreducible minimum" in Jewish politics.

5) Local self-government and mixed Jewish-Arab municipal and rural coun-
cils, on a small scale and as numerous as possible, are the only realistic
political measures that can eventually lead to the political emancipation
of Palestine. It is still not too late.

Two years later Arendt wrote of the nonnationalist tradition in Zionism
and the danger of nationalism for small nations relating to military and
economic dependency. To continue support from abroad Israel might
find itself in the "unenviable position of being forced to create emer-
gencies, that is, forced into a policy of aggressiveness and expansion."
Arendt concluded "The birth of a nation in the midst of our century
may be a great event; it certainly is a dangerous event" (Arendt 1978,
221–22).

Of course, many other facets of Arendt's thought bear analysis, and
she herself became so discouraged about the state of Jewish discussion
that she virtually ceased writing on Jewish topics in 1966. Like most
Jews, though, when catastrophe threatened she rallied behind Israel.
Celebrating the victory in the Six Day War of June 1967 she wrote to
Mary McCarthy, "Any real catastrophe in Israel would affect me more
deeply than almost anything else." In the Yom Kippur War in October
1973 Arendt feared that Israel might this time be destroyed, and she
offered financial and moral assistance. Arendt the nonnationalist was in
the same boat with other dissenting Jews in fearing another holocaust.
What Arendt did not know was the extent of destruction possible, for
Israel had compelled the United States to provide a massive shipment
of conventional weapons to Israel by threatening to use nuclear weapons
against their adversaries in the Middle East.

With her death in 1975 she was also spared knowledge of the inevitable consequences of an occupation that has now entered its third
decade: consistent violations of human rights, including torture and
murder. Just ten years after her death some Israeli writers heralded the
arrival of Israel as a leading global arms exporter, the thought of which
would have horrified Arendt. To be sure, Arendt's critical analysis continues today in such writers as Noam Chomsky and Israel Shahak,
though the opposition and its power are even more concentrated now
than they were in Arendt's time. Forty years after her most powerful
essay on the critical issues of Jewish life, Arendt's judgments seem more
than accurate; they were and are prophetic.

## SOLIDARITY AND THEOLOGICAL CRITIQUE

Though Arendt was thoroughly secular in her outlook, others in
the hidden tradition struggled toward a religious vision in literary and

philosophical frameworks. This is true of two figures about whom Arendt wrote, Franz Kafka and Walter Benjamin. We might say that from the beginning of the hidden tradition a dialectical tension existed between secular and religious critique most exemplified in Walter Benjamin's "Treatise on History." Here he suggests the possible interplay of political revolution and theology, as in this statement: "Our experience forbids us to conceive history in fundamentally atheological terms, however little one ought to try to write it in theological terms." This tension of politics and theology allowed Jewish intellectuals of the hidden tradition to investigate the world beyond the confines of Jewish particularity without absolutizing the secular. In retrospect, this search bore great fruit in both realms though often at great emotional and physical cost. The loneliness and isolation of Kafka and Benjamin, of Arendt herself, testify to the difficulty of living between two worlds, at home in neither.

The experience of Holocaust has brought this sense of isolation and abandonment to a deeper level and the dialect of secular and religious critique has collapsed into a militancy, both secular and religious, ·that reinforces the isolation it hoped to end. Empowered, the Jewish people feel more embattled than generations previous to the Holocaust. Though Israel is one of the most formidable military powers in the world, the Jewish perception is that it is continually on the brink of holocaust. This accounts for the curious, one might even say blasphemous, comparison of Adolf Hitler and Yasir Arafat, one a genocidal murderer of the Jewish people, the other considered by those outside the Jewish community as a moderate in the Middle East. The liturgy of destruction rehearsed by Holocaust theologians again plays a major role here; it does not help us to understand the history we are creating today and thus distorts the question of what it means to be faithful as a Jew within empowerment (Ellis 1987, 1–4).

Movements of renewal within the Jewish community speaking in identifiably religious language as well as a revived and transformed hidden tradition are crucial to challenge the dominance of Holocaust theology. The hidden tradition, especially, needs to maintain its link with secular language and critique as it begins to explore religious language and activity in a new light. That which was latent in Kafka, Benjamin, and Arendt comes to the fore in a dialectical tension responding to changed circumstances and historical configurations.

There is little question that the major transformation of religious language and activity in the West and around the world since the Holocaust is found in Christian political and liberation theology, with its emphasis on critical thought and solidarity in the struggle for justice. Here a fount of images and possibilities opens to the Jewish people. Such an exploration is difficult because of the history we have been through together, but political and liberation theology, especially, provide an opening to understand the struggles and suffering of those around the world. For they take seriously the question of suffering and often express it in a conceptual framework—Exodus, the prophetic, idolatry—bequeathed to the world by the Jewish people. This allows us to see our own history in another, less isolationist, perspective. At the same time, it calls forth a critical understanding of our own empowerment. The issue of solidarity raised by political and liberation theology forces us to move beyond a theology that no longer describes the history we are creating (Ellis 1978, 67–90).

For both Jew and Christian the question of solidarity begins with the Jewish experience of suffering in the Holocaust and the Christian response. Johann Baptist Metz's essay "Christians and Jews after Auschwitz" is crucial here. Metz, a German Catholic theologian, sees Auschwitz as a turning point rather than an end point in Christian-Jewish relations. He asks Christians, "Will we actually allow it to be the end point, the disruption which it really was, the catastrophe of our history, out of which we can find a way only through a radical change of direction achieved via new standards of action? Or will we see it only as a monstrous accident within history but not effecting history's course?" Clearly for Metz the Holocaust is the turning point in Christian history and Christian-Jewish relations. To the question of whether a Christian can pray after Auschwitz, Metz responds in the affirmative because people prayed in Auschwitz (Metz 1981, 18–19).

The root of Jewish-Christian ecumenism comes into focus as a common journey forged in suffering: "We Christians can never again go back behind Auschwitz: to go beyond Auschwitz, if we see clearly, is impossible for us of ourselves. It is possible only together with the victims of Auschwitz." Even theodicy is challenged: Metz considers as blasphemy Christian belief structures that are "initiated outside this catastrophe or on some level above it." Again the reference is to Jewish suffering and meaning that can only be invoked as it was within Auschwitz and in dialogue with the heirs of Auschwitz (Metz 1981, 19).

For Metz, forging an alliance with the victims of Auschwitz means in the first place the end of persecution of Jews by Christians. But it also means something else: "If any persecution were to take place in the future, it could only be a persecution of both together, of Jews *and*

Christians—*as it was in the beginning*. It is well known that the early persecutions of Christians were also persecutions of the Jews. Because both groups refused to recognize the Roman Emperor as God, thus calling into question the foundation of Rome's political religion, they were together branded as atheists and haters of the human race and were persecuted unto death." Thus Metz accomplishes the important task of placing the Jewish victims at the center of Christian consciousness and resistance as well as inviting contemporary Jews and Christians to accompany one another in the difficult project of social critique and transformation (Metz 1981, 20).

Gustavo Gutiérrez, the Peruvian theologian of liberation, citing the work of Metz in relation to Europe and North America, asks the Jewish people to take the next step: to accompany others in their suffering in the present. In the conclusion of his book *On Job: God-Talk and the Suffering of the Innocent,* Gutiérrez writes of the Holocaust as an "inescapable challenge to Christian conscience and an inexcusable reproach to the silence of many Christians in the face of that dreadful event." The question of human suffering and God's presence is an essential one, but for Latin Americans the question is not, How are we to do theology after Auschwitz?

> The reason is that in Latin America we are still experiencing every day the violation of human rights, murder, and the torture that we find so blameworthy in the Jewish holocaust of World War II. Our task here is to find the words with which to talk about God in the midst of the starvation of millions, the humiliation of races regarded as inferior, discrimination against women, especially women who are poor, systematic social injustice, a persistent high rate of infant mortality, those who simply "disappear" or are deprived of their freedom, the sufferings of peoples who are struggling for their right to live, the exiles and the refugees, terrorism of every kind, and the corpse-filled common graves of *Ayacucho*. What we must deal with is not the past but, unfortunately, a cruel present and a dark tunnel with no apparent end. (Gutiérrez 1987, 102)

Rather, the question asked in Latin America is, "How do we do theology *while Ayacucho lasts*? How are we to speak of the God of life when cruel murder on a massive scale goes on in 'the corner of the dead'?" (Gutiérrez 1987, 101, 102).

Metz and Gutiérrez suggest the way to lessen Jewish isolation and preoccupation with Jewish suffering is through accompaniment and activity on behalf of those who suffer today. Could it be that our particularity would once again lend depth to the struggle and hope?

Still, if Christians cannot move into the future without the victims of Auschwitz, and if the theological question today revolves around the corner of the dead, then the ecumenical project has a critical edge for Jews as well as Christians. For we are contributing to the corner of the dead, and Jews cannot move forward without the very victims we are creating. To paraphrase Metz, the challenge might be stated thus: We Jews can never go back behind empowerment. To go beyond empowerment, if we see clearly, is impossible for us by ourselves. It is possible only with the victims of our empowerment.

These are hard words for Jews to hear and speak; they suggest a culpability in the liturgy of destruction that the ghetto scribes could hardly imagine. This new and terrible scripture bears recitation to our children. But the hidden tradition of critical thought as well as a new-found solidarity with those who once oppressed us may also allow us to transform our empowerment into the path of liberation. In this light the central questions facing the Jewish community are these: How are we to do theology in the face of the Jewish Holocaust while *Ayacucho* continues? How are we contributing to the corner of the dead? How can we move beyond complicity into a solidarity that is confessional, transformative, and actively engaged in the pursuit of justice? As in any movement outward toward those who are suffering, it is at the same moment a movement toward the deepest themes of Jewish community life: ethics, the prophetic, and the refusal of idolatry. Hence the task of a Jewish theology of liberation: to join with others in the ongoing struggle for human dignity and justice with the hope that we can become what we are called to be.

## References

Arendt, Hannah. 1978. *The Jew as Pariah: Jewish Identity and Politics in the Modern Age.* Ed. Ron H. Feldman. New York: Grove Press.

Ellis, Marc H. 1987. *Toward a Jewish Theology of Liberation.* Maryknoll: Orbis Books.

———. 1990. *Beyond Innocence and Redemption: Confronting the Holocaust and Israeli Power.* San Francisco: Harper San Francisco.

Feldman, Ron H. 1978. Introduction. In *The Jew as Pariah: Jewish Identity and Politics in the Modern Age.* Hannah Arendt. New York: Grove Press.

Feuerlicht, Roberta Strauss. 1983. *The Fate of Jews: A People Torn between Israeli Power and Jewish Ethics.* New York: Time Books.

Greenberg, Irving. 1977. Cloud of smoke, pillar of fire: Judaism, Christianity and modernism after the Holocaust. In *Auschwitz: Beginning of a New Era?* Ed. Eva Fleischner. New York: KATV.

———. 1985. Some lessons from Bitburg. *Perspectives* (May).

Gutiérrez, Gustavo. 1987. *On Job: God-Talk and the Suffering of the Innocent.* Trans. Matthew J. O'Connell. Maryknoll: Orbis Books.

Metz, Johann Baptist. 1981. *The Emerging Church: The Future of Christianity in a Postbourgeois World.* Trans. Peter Mann. New York: Crossroad.

Roskies, David G. 1984. *Against the Apocalypse: Responses to Catastrophe in Modern Jewish Culture.* Cambridge: Harvard Univ. Press.

Rubenstein, Richard. 1975. *The Cunning of History: Mass Death and the American Future.* New York: Harper & Row.

Scholem, Gershom. 1978. Eichmann in Jerusalem. In *The Jew as Pariah: Jewish Identity and Politics in the Modern Age.* Hannah Arendt. New York: Grove Press.

# PART TWO

## DISCIPLINES
## IN DIALOGUE

# 6

# New Church, New Ministries

## Richard Shaull

During more than four decades spent in the practice of mission and reflection on it, I have been primarily concerned about the revitalization of faith, the resurrection of the church, and the dynamic involvement of Christians in movements for social transformation. I can now see that all of these things are happening on a scale I had never imagined but not as the result of efforts made by me and those with whom I have been associated nor in the groups on which we had counted. Christianity is getting a new lease on life in the "church of the poor," the "church of women," the sanctuary movement, and other similar groups.

When oppressed people become aware of their oppression, take up the struggle for liberation, and reconnect with their religious heritage, they often find that it takes on new meaning and vitality. The Bible speaks a new and compelling word and comes to play an important role in orienting their life journey. Faith is reborn as they live a new experience of transcendence in the midst of daily life and struggle. Their lives are renewed and sustained in a new community of faith, and the Christian story becomes their story as they experience joy and hope in the midst of conflict and persecution. Because of these developments we may find ourselves today at the beginning of a new era in Christian history, a new *kairos* in which the Holy Spirit is present once again as the spirit of novelty and creativity.

When I look at the conditions under which this rebirth is occurring, several things stand out.

1. This movement of the Spirit is taking place on what we might call a new missionary frontier: among those whom the Latin Americans identify as *el nuevo sujeto historico,* the new historical subject. Through the popular movements in the third world and the feminist movement here and elsewhere, a new social class is emerging. Those who have been the most exploited and oppressed are becoming the protagonists of history. They are the ones who have the vision, the energy, and the commitment needed to create a new society and open a new future for the world. Those who have been most deprived are willing to risk death in order to lay the foundation for an economic order in which the resources of each nation can be used to create conditions for life for all, beginning at the bottom. Those who have been denied a place in structures of domination are envisioning a society in which power relations will be radically changed, moving from the bottom up rather than the top down, a society in which women and men learn how to relate in terms of mutual empowerment. The frontier of mission has shifted from certain geographical areas to a social class. And the rediscovery of the biblical story as the story of liberation, of the God of the Bible as the God who appears in history as the liberator of slaves, and of Jesus of Nazareth as the Messiah of the poor who inaugurates a new kingdom of justice belonging to the poor and marginal, provides the basis for a dynamic Christian presence on this frontier.

2. A new church is emerging *in the midst of this new social class,* a church born out of the suffering and struggle of oppressed people and those who stand with them. The Holy Spirit is present in a dramatic way among those struggling for justice and willing to give their lives to that cause. In and through them the Spirit may be saying something quite important to us about where the true church comes into being. For in these small communities striving for life against the forces of death in society, women and men hear the biblical message and find that it speaks to them. They have a new experience of the presence of God and come to know a richness of life together that sustains them day by day.

3. Once again the church is becoming what it is called to be at all times: *a sign of the coming kingdom, the "first-fruits" of the new age.* In a world so organized that power is concentrated in the hands of a few men at the top, leaving the vast majority of people powerless and pushing us to the brink of disaster, those who have been deprived of power are envisioning and struggling for a society in which women and men can learn to relate to each other in a more human way, to

empower each other and take increasing control of their lives and destiny, individually and collectively. In the new communities of faith this quality of life in relationship is being forged. This is the amazing reality found so often in the Christian base communities as well as the "church of women." These two movements complement and support each other. In the words of Elisabeth Schüssler Fiorenza:

> The "church of the poor" and the "church of women" must be recovered at the same time, if "solidarity from below" is to become a reality for the whole community of Jesus again. As a feminist vision the *basilea* vision of Jesus calls all women without exception to wholeness and selfhood, as well as to solidarity with those women who are the impoverished, the maimed and outcasts of our society and church. . . . The woman-identified man, Jesus, called forth a discipleship of equals that still needs to be discovered and realized by women and men today. (Fiorenza 1983, 153–54)

## MINISTRY: VOCATION OR PROFESSION?

You and I, whether or not we belong to one or the other of these two communities of faith, need to ask ourselves, What is the Holy Spirit saying to us today in and through these developments? How can we, situated wherever we are, participate as dynamically as possible in this process of creation of new life in community?

Here I want to focus on one aspect only: *the missionary or ministerial vocation*. In my contact with base communities in Latin America, I have been struck by the fact that so many of them began as the result of the presence there of one or two persons, usually priests or nuns, who had a vision of mutual empowerment and were willing to spend years if necessary until they found and brought together a small nucleus who shared and responded to that vision.

I recently took part in a program of theological education sponsored by the Departamento Ecumenico de Investigaciones in San Jose, Costa Rica, a *Taller* (workshop) for women and men from many countries who are now working at this ministry as enablers and coordinators of these communities. The members of this group included a few priests and a number of nuns, but the majority was made up of lay people who had emerged at the grass roots as community leaders or university graduates who had made a vocational decision to work for the *provecto de los pobres* (the project of the poor). What most impressed me was the fact that all of them were committed to—and were living out—a new type of ministry. *They saw their vocation as that of doing everything possible to develop and sustain faith communities that enable and empower the poor in their struggle to emerge as subjects,* and many of them were willingly paying a high price to follow it.

I am convinced that the development of a church of this type in North America will depend to no small degree on the emergence of a new ministry with a similar vocational commitment. But how can this happen? For decades I assumed that I could best work for the rebirth of the church by dedicating my energies to the preparation of its future ministers in one or another of our major centers of theological education. But it has not worked out that way for me in Brazil or in the United States. I hoped to contribute to the preparation of a new generation of ministers committed to the renewal of the church. What I did not take seriously enough was the fact that the problem lay not just in the lack of a clear sense of vocation on the part of seminary students but in the fundamental conception of ministry as it has been developed in our churches and the way it has been institutionalized. *Ministry as it is structured within the religious institution functions to block rather than create space for the new reality of faith and community now beginning to appear among oppressed people.*

In the church of the poor and the church of women, a community of faith comes into existence as believers in Jesus Christ take up the struggle for liberation in an attempt to overcome the present structures of the dominant order. But the church as institution has functioned for more than fifteen hundred years as an integral part of that order. In that position it, like any other major institution, is concerned about its own preservation and growth, not about death and resurrection. Its seminaries are part of that structure and function in the same way. And most of those who decide to go to seminary and become ministers, especially young people just out of college, are thinking of *serving* that institution, not *subverting* it. With rare exceptions those who serve the institution in this way are the ones who move into positions of responsibility and prestige in it. As I traveled across the country meeting with groups in the Presbyterian church concerned about changing U.S. policy in Central America, I came to realize that rarely do pastors take the initiative in forming such groups or even show interest in them before they become well established, if then.

The problem is even more serious if we take into account, in the church of the poor and of women, the work of the Spirit creating a community of equals, in which especially those at the bottom emerge as subjects and learn to empower each other. For the whole ethos of the ministry leads the minister to move in the opposite direction because of a number of historical factors, the existence of which we recognize but somehow rarely take into account in our planning.

The church developed in a historical era in which those at the top of the ladder in the political and religious worlds were thought to belong to the world of the divine. Years ago Arend van Leeuwen in his study of *Christianity in World History* called our attention to the nature of ontocratic societies, in which rulers were considered to be more than human because they participated in the eternal realm of being. This ontocratic idea has long since been undermined when applied to kings or other secular rulers. But it has not completely disappeared in the church, where those at the top are seen as representatives of God, the priest has power over the divine in the sacraments, and the Protestant minister proclaims divine truth from the pulpit. Even if the clergy do nothing to encourage this attitude, many of the faithful still function on these terms.

Early Christianity developed in a society organized hierarchically. Early on patterns of organization developed in the Roman Empire were adopted by the church; later the same thing happened in relation to feudal society. To this day the position of the minister in the church is partly defined by this history.

In the Reformation of the sixteenth century the affirmation of the priesthood of all believers was part of a theological approach aimed at undermining this type of authority. But the Reformers bought the whole cultural package of their time, and the pastor continued to exercise power and organize the church around himself and a small elite. In Calvinist circles the minister as preacher of the word continued to have special authority. And as Protestantism did not succeed very well in providing its ministers with a clearly defined role in society, they have tended to see themselves in terms of the professional roles popular in a particular time and place.

As a result, in Protestant circles at least, the minister is now a *middle-class professional*. The professional mentality is an integral part of our Western liberal culture organized, as it is, on the principle of "boundary management" or "turf." Society is made up of many autonomous zones of jurisdiction, each with its own language and order, whose members are committed to maintaining, defending, and extending their realm. Professionals have been specially trained to solve problems and provide services for others in the particular area in which they are experts. Their personal identity and sense of importance and worth are defined by their position within that structure. Moreover their success is measured by their ability to be upwardly mobile, which means not only to improve their economic position but to occupy a position of greater prestige in the community and influence a larger number of people.

Given the pervasiveness of this value system in our society, we should hardly be surprised to find that ministers trained to be professionals see the local congregation as their turf, where they feel most successful and satisfied when they deprive others of the opportunity to take responsibility and become subjects.

When this way of life enters crisis, the problem becomes more acute. Young people facing a deep crisis of personal identity and unsure of their place in the world—a surprising number of whom seem to find their way to seminary—tend to find security in a professional role. The more precarious the ego, the more important it is to have a clearly defined role, learn professional techniques, and use them. For such people nothing is more frightening than the emergence in their congregations of people—especially women and socially marginal people—who claim the right to be subjects in a community of equals.

When our mainline Protestant churches established missions among the poor at home and abroad, they took with them this system of values, the professional ethos, and the emphasis on upward mobility. Seminaries were often filled with men who could not find a professional space for themselves in the secular world but had these same expectations. When they became pastors, some of them defended the pastoral turf with a vengeance, even when it meant excluding the most intelligent and committed young people from any active role in the life of the congregation.

## THE FUTURE OF MINISTRY

If we take these factors into account I believe we can see the dimensions of the problem before us and what is involved in developing a new ministry for a new church. To further the discussion, I suggest the following.

1. As I mentioned earlier, the church of the poor began in Latin America when a few priests, nuns, and women and men from some of the professions felt called to a new type of ministry and proceeded to live it out. They were grasped by a vision of a new community of faith in which the poorest might become subjects as they learned to share with and empower each other. Motivated by this vision, they went to

the poor in their neighborhoods and lived and worked with them until this new quality of life in relationship captured the imagination of a few and became a reality.

This, I believe, is of central importance as a first step. In Latin America those who had this vision often spent years finding a few people who were open to it. In this country at the present time we may discover that at the base more people than we imagine are ready for it. But we lack people interested in and prepared to perform the ministerial task of providing resources for them. Recent efforts to develop base communities among Hispanics in the South Bronx got almost immediate response from a number of parishioners throughout the barrio. What was not forthcoming was a core of people willing to work with them, especially when the parish priests did not support the project. Time and again when I have met with groups in local churches or communities working on Central American issues, I have found the same desire for a new quality of life in community and a lack of people available to facilitate its development.

At the end of the last century, when North American Christians became aware of a new missionary frontier, small groups of young men and women felt themselves called to this missionary vocation and got together to study what was happening around the world, define what this new vocation involved, prepare themselves for it, and figure out ways to fulfill their calling. In relation to the new challenge before us, I think that there is a call for something similar.

2. I am convinced that theological education should have its base and focus, not in seminaries, but in the new communities emerging among the poor and marginal, the church of women and those involved in Witness for Peace and other groups coming together around peace and justice issues. Taking into account what is happening with theologians in Latin America and in the women's movement here, clearly the most authentic theological thinking goes on in the midst of praxis, as the marginal oppressed struggle for life. In these communities many new ministries are emerging and those who exercise them are eager for opportunities to study the Bible and the theological tradition and to learn how to analyze what is happening in society around them. In the last few years, I have found more excitement about the study of theology and more profound thinking about the gospel going on in such groups than with seminary students with whom I have been in contact. If we are really interested in preparing women and men for ministry, we have here an extraordinary opportunity we should no longer ignore.

Moreover, in these new grass-roots communities, the Pauline vision of a church in which each member has a *charisma* (gift of the Spirit) for building up the body is becoming a reality. This is something we often spoke about in the church renewal movement while maintaining congregations directed by the minister and a few lay people. But the church emerging among the poor and marginal, a church of equals who are learning to empower each other, can be a church only as those with this rich diversity of gifts for ministry are recognized, trained, and given an opportunity to serve. In the face of this new development it no longer makes sense to concentrate all efforts in theological education on the training of a small number of professional ministers while ignoring the needs and interests of those who are the source of the life of the church at its base.

3. From among such people, trained for and exercising a dynamic ministry at the base, the Holy Spirit will raise up a new type of minister who will have a special vocation for building up the faith community, in continuity with what has been done across the centuries by priest, pastor, and missionary. In the new church, a small number of women and men will be needed who will take upon themselves this project of giving shape to a community of equals and make it the passion of their lives.

Some will be ordained, others will not. Some will have this as their full-time involvement; others will work at it part-time. Some will receive salary for it; others will be nonstipendiary. They will work at a variety of tasks that contribute to building up the base communities and preparing their members for ministry, recognizing the most urgent tasks calling for their efforts in a particular time and place. Their sense of personal identity as well as of direction and purpose in life will come, not from the position they hold as professionals, but from their sense of the historical importance of the project in which they and the people among whom they work are engaged.

Given the image of ministry common in the church today, we can hardly assume that young people who decide to go to seminary are the ones called to this new ministry. Nor can we assume that those who have a special vocation of this sort will recognize their calling or decide to go to seminary. The emerging new church may well find it necessary to choose those in its midst who can best serve in a ministry of empowerment and lay that call before them. We should also recognize that those who do respond to such a call are not likely to find that our seminaries, as they now function, are capable of preparing them for ministry. The emergence of a new ministry calls for new ventures in theological education.

4. As we find and train this ministry we will also discover that the most urgent theological task before us is that of *re-creating* a two-thousand-year-old tradition. Neoorthodoxy made a tremendous contribution to the life of the church because it not only put us back in touch with that heritage of faith but it helped us focus theological reflection on it. Thus it prepared the ground for the creative task now ahead of us.

As I have worked with women and men whose faith is being renewed in the midst of their struggle for a more human life and for justice, I find that they keep raising profound theological questions with a seriousness not often found in academic circles. But when I attempt to teach them theology by repeating language and concepts from the past, they lose no time in declaring that all this has little meaning for them. Only as I attempt to bring that heritage into dialogue with their situation and express it in a new language is there a chance that what it has to offer will be grasped and become a source of orientation and of life for them. As they pursue their spiritual journey they are not inclined to fit themselves into a conceptual system presented to them as the truth. What is important is to find resources to put their thought and lives together in a meaningful way. They are eager to find such orientation and may be willing to look for it in the Bible and the teachings of the church. But that heritage speaks to them only as the theologian is living in their midst and has discovered how to express it in ways that open new possibilities of understanding and action for them. A new ministry challenges us to take upon ourselves the exciting and formidable task of theological re-creation.

## References

Fiorenza, Elisabeth Schüssler. 1983. *In Memory of Her*. New York: Crossroad.

van Leeuwen, Arend. 1964. *Christianity in World History*. London: Edinburgh House Press.

# 7

# Catholicity, Inculturation, and Liberation Theology: The Case of Leonardo Boff

## Harvey G. Cox

The silencing of the Brazilian Franciscan theologian in 1985 reveals a lot about the current status of liberation theology and its ongoing lover's quarrel with the institutional church. The disciplining of Boff was directed not against a single theologian but against the entire theology of liberation movement. The "unsilencing" of Boff in the spring of 1986, although it was a welcome move, did not resolve issues raised by that contest between the Sacred Congregation for the Doctrine of the Faith and the movement Leonardo Boff represents. The renewed disciplining of Boff in 1991 suggests that the issues are deep and pervasive.

Some have asked me why a Protestant theologian, a Baptist in particular, should be concerned about Leonardo Boff or about a movement that is as characteristically Catholic in so many aspects as liberation theology, especially in its Latin American form. It is a legitimate question, and I would like to underline that it is precisely *because* of my free church, biblically centered, evangelical formation that I find liberation theology particularly attractive. It is a movement, after all, based on small base communities, "local congregations" one might say, meeting around the Bible, trying to understand the will of God for the lives of the people in that local community and in the wider world. It is a highly christological movement based on a recognition that God has come as the liberator and God remains in our midst in the person and spirit of

Jesus Christ. Consequently, liberation theology resonates strongly with the kind of spirituality on which I was raised. I also want to say, lest any of my fellow Baptists begin to get too proud about it, that often the liberation theologians and the base communities are actually *doing* what we have been *talking* about but not always doing for many years. So I frankly welcome this movement, and I cannot talk or write about it from a strictly neutral point of view.

## THE MARKS OF THE CHURCH

I believe that the basic issue raised by the case of Leonardo Boff is that of ecclesiology, the nature of the church. Notice that he had written a number of books, by my count, about a dozen, and another dozen major articles before his disciplining by Rome. It was only when a particular book was published, *Church: Charisma and Power,* that his invitation to Rome arrived with an Air Italia ticket enclosed. It was only when he raised the issue of ecclesiology, and when he applied the insights of liberation theology to the structure of the church itself, its government and its use of authority, that suddenly he found himself silenced.

Boff was silenced because he bears witness to the fact that liberation theology is not something the church can simply direct *ad extram*—(its prophetic criticism of an unjust society) although it certainly is that; it also has to do with a radical reformation of the church itself. Traditionally the marks of the true church are four: *one, holy, apostolic,* and *catholic.* The debate between Leonardo Boff and Cardinal Ratzinger and his supporters has to do with the question of the apostolicity, catholicity, oneness, and holiness of the church. Liberation theologians ask, what do all these words mean today? I would like here to discuss only one of the four, the issue of *catholicity,* with but a preliminary word about the closely linked notion of the apostolicity of the church.

Apostolicity means that the church is the *Christian* church only when it can trace itself in some manner to the actual ministry and life of Jesus Christ and his disciples. This connection is what *makes* the church Christian; it is what makes it "apostolic." Traditionally, of course, this connection is presented in terms of "apostolic succession." In Catholic theology it has been interpreted in terms of the appointment of Peter and of the subsequent generations of popes and bishops. In the liberation theology perspective, however, the church is apostolic insofar as it is *doing* what *Jesus Christ* himself *did,* continuing his life and witness. This is a *functional* understanding of apostolicity. In fact, using a term liberation theologians like to use, the church's "project" (*el projecto*) creates the continuity between the apostolic church and today's church. The project of Jesus Christ—his life purpose—was the announcement and embodiment of the reign of God. This was also the project of the disciples, and it is the project to which the church is called today. Only insofar as the church enters into and shares that project can it be called truly "apostolic."

Some people might say, Why bicker about this? Why ask whether a church is apostolic or not? But both for the critics of liberation theology and for liberation theologians themselves, this laissez-faire attitude will not do. There are many conflicting claims to what "Christian" means. We *do* need norms, some way to make judgments about what we can legitimately call Christian, and what we cannot. Otherwise, where do we go? What about the Aryan Church of True Christianity, which is growing up in the Midwest these days "to save the white race"? What about the racist offshoots of the Dutch Reformed Church of South Africa? What about the Church of Scientology? There are many movements in the United States that call themselves "Christian." Is there some way that we can make some discrimination among them on the basis of apostolicity? That question is important, and the debate between liberation theologians and the position represented by Rome is not just theoretical. Let us now turn to the issue of "catholicity" because I think this is the central one raised by global cultural pluralism.

When I was in Latin America in 1985 doing the research for the book I later wrote on the Boff case, I talked with a number of Brazilians both inside and outside the church. All insisted that the Boff case did not have much to do with "Marxist influence" or with heresy. What was really at issue, they said, was whether a "Eurocentric" form of theology and church governance could make theological and ecclesiastical judgments on a Latin American and specifically Brazilian form of Christianity and church organization. From that perspective of these Latin Americans, *l'affaire Boff* was yet another example of European cultural hegemony and religious imperialism, of not allowing the Brazilian church to be Brazilian. An Indian Catholic cardinal once said that "the Catholic Church is neither Latin nor Greek nor Slav but universal, and unless the church can become Indian in India, Chinese in China, Japanese in Japan, she will never reveal her authentically Catholic character." *Catholic,* in this reading, must mean culturally inclusive, present in a diversity of cultures. A truly catholic church will not only allow but will encourage diverse forms of indigenous Christianity.

This all seems increasingly self-evident, but it does not resolve the issue. Eventually one does have to have some norms for distinguishing the blooming of a thousand flowers from the growth of poison ivy. Even though such judgments may be difficult to make, we cannot avoid making them. Even if we eventually decide to "tolerate" groups that spuriously claim to be Christian, simply avoiding judgment is not possible. This is a position on which Boff and Ratzinger agree. What then is the difference?

For Cardinal Ratzinger catholicity is a *quality* that already exists in its fullness in the Roman Catholic Church. It is of the essence of that church, the name by which it is most commonly known. Therefore it is a cherished treasure and an invaluable asset; it is a gift from God which the Catholic church is called upon to share with other religious bodies and eventually with the whole world. In this view, to become Catholic is to become a part of the existing visible Catholic church, to become a part of its values, its stories, its governance: to participate in its culture.

For the liberation theologians, on the other hand, catholicity is a gift of God, but it is also an unaccomplished task; it has an unfinished, promissory, even eschatological dimension. Therefore in our age of global cultural pluralism catholicity can only be realized when the church is de-Europeanized, that is, released from its captivity to one particular culture, so that it can enter fully into others.

While in Brazil I also learned a very helpful word: *desnortificacão*. I like it much better than "demythologization." It means "denorthification," and it implies that Christianity has been overdefined by the Northern Hemisphere and is now ready for a release from that captivity. For the liberation theologians, therefore, catholicity is present in the Catholic church more as a promise than as a reality, more as a goal than as an accomplished fact. Achieving catholicity will require *desnortificacão*.

The nature of catholicity was the subject of the conversation Leonardo Boff had with Cardinal Ratzinger inside the confines of the Sacred Congregation for the Doctrine of the Faith. If we can believe Boff's account, they talked about exactly this issue: to what extent the Catholic church is the church of Christ; to what extent it might not be, fully and completely; to what extent other bodies might also share in this catholicity. From Boff's perspective, catholicity must not only be *shared;* it must also be *sought,* and this was the root of his disagreement with the prefect.

At the heart of the dispute over catholicity is the question of the proper relationship of the particular to the universal. Considering the far-reaching implications of this debate, it is important to recall that in the eighteenth and nineteenth centuries, the Enlightenment critics of Christianity berated it for *not being universal enough,* for its specious claim to universality when—they insisted—it was really a particular, narrow, and dogmatic religion. They still held, however, that it was important to have a universal, inclusive, spiritual system and they believed that they themselves had found the *truly* universal religion in the allegedly simple and uncorrupted faith of the indigenous peoples of the new world, who were (they believed) untouched by priestcraft and dogma. They found universality in "natural religion." The quest for universality continued to be a part of the Enlightenment dream.

In the twentieth century the tables have been turned. After the ravages of fascism and totalitarianism, the critics now indict Christianity not for being too particular but for being *too universal:* It is accused of being both a cause and an effect of that obsessive modern need to homogenize, control, and level out differences. It feeds the drive to include everything in one inclusive system, a tendency some critics claim showed its most horrid face in Hitler's *Gleichshaltung* ("integration"). Thus were the terms of the debate inverted from the nineteenth to the twentieth century. The critics of Christianity's universalism no longer contend that it is merely a disguised form of particularism but that the very goal of universality itself is incipiently totalitarian. One can find this reproach especially among poststructuralists and the followers of Michel Foucault, and it has been picked up by some of the feminist critics as well. There is a suspicion that all universalizing systems disguise a hidden imperialism. So consequently Christianity is rejected, not because it is too particular, but because it strives to be universal, and that is the real danger.

It takes little effort to point out the contradictions in these two criticisms, but Christianity itself has sometimes contributed to the muddle. Its mistaken solution to the perennially pressing problem of universal faith and particular cultures for Western Catholicism and even Protestant Christianity was to identify one culture as normative. Thus Hellenistic European culture, which provided the cultural vehicle for one (albeit dominant) form of Christianity became normative. Even within our own time, for example, Ugandans were expected to celebrate the Mass in Latin, Japanese were taught to understand the logic of the *Summa Theologiae,* and some French Catholics in the early twentieth century coined the phrase, *"La foi c'est l'Europe: l'Europe c'est la foi"* (Europe is the faith; the faith is Europe). We have picked up a little of their language in the phrase "Western Christian civilization." This phrase conveys the idea that there is something essentially Western about Christianity (and maybe something essentially Christian about the West). If that is the case perhaps we should be honest and simply settle for a Western religious particularism, a kind of Euro-American Shinto. But this would require us to drop the whole idea of catholicity from our understanding of the church. It does not seem to be the solution.

How do the theologians of liberation deal with the issue of a universal faith and particular cultures? They begin by suggesting that the catholicity of the church is not an existing essence to be extended. Rather, like the reign of God, it is somehow both a divine gift and a goal of human striving. Further, the church's own catholicity—however partial or incomplete—is meant to be a sign or sacrament of the wholeness that God intends for the entire world. Therefore the church cannot itself be truly catholic while the civil societies of this world, whose peoples make up the church, exclude and marginalize minorities, women, and others by depriving them of full participation. Jesus' own entourage, which is the embryo of the church, brought together representatives of the rival factions and alienated peoples of his own day, including women and tax collectors. It was itself a sign of the reign he was introducing. But the reign would only come to pass when the poor were vindicated, the prisoners were freed, and all the nations of the earth could discard their swords and chariots. That is, the church's catholicity and the coming of the reign of God are mutually dependent on each other.

## INCULTURATION VS. INCARNATION

This takes us to the current debate about inculturation. How does the church insert itself into such varied cultures and still retain some element of oneness of catholicity, some visible unity?

It sometimes comes as a surprise to learn that liberation theologians are suspicious of many of the current arguments that urge the church to "inculturate" itself. But their apprehensiveness is understandable. It arises from their experience with the "underclass" people of the various cultures including the ones with which they work. In this work they have learned that *culture* is not a neutral term, that culture *itself can be despotic.* Culture can be used to exclude and bully people. Many Latin American theologians have seen their own people hurt by repressive measures taken by authoritarian governments in the name of such potent symbols such as *homeland* or *Western Christian civilization* or *patriotic duty,* all cultural terms. They have learned to be suspicious of advocates of inculturation who do not recognize that culture can be used to manipulate powerless people, drawing on their folk beliefs and pious practices to keep them quiescent.

But liberation theologians also recognize that no faith, especially Christianity, can exist without some cultural vehicle. So their question becomes, "How can one be *selective* about the *mode* of insertion or inculturation so that one does not give a blanket endorsement to those cultural elements that are oppressive?"

For liberation theologians, as I read them on this issue, the answer is christological. The model of Jesus' interaction with this culture provides the essential starting point: *apostolicity guides catholicity.* Jesus was deeply steeped in the religion and culture of his own people. He was not counter-cultural despite the T-shirt from the 1960s that said, "Jesus was a hippie." But he did not hesitate to point out in his teaching and preaching how the religious elites of his day were *misusing* their religious inheritance. Jesus, in fact, invoked very old religious and cultural traditions such as the jubilee year, which called for the forgiveness of debts and mortgages. He regularly quoted the Law and the Prophets to his religious critics. He did not either uncritically embrace culture or uncritically reject it; rather, he used it against its distortions. He drew on the Psalms and the ritual law to expose those who were exploiting them for their own gain. "It is written, 'My house shall be a house of prayer' but you have made it a den of robbers" (Luke 19:46).

Because the word *inculturation* is general and uncritical, liberation theologians, in keeping with their emphasis on the model of Jesus, often suggest that *incarnation* is a better metaphor of how the church should be present in culture. Incarnation calls to mind the example of how Jesus himself was often in conflict with culture. It reminds us that cultures are themselves in conflict. The Duvalier family regime in Haiti clung to power for several decades in part by exploiting such popular spiritual practices as voodoo. Men still subject women to subservience in most parts of the world by appealing to cultural images of "womanhood." Racism is an integral part of the culture in many places. There is often a kind of innocence in the way some people advocate "inculturating" or "indigenizing" Christianity or the church without recognizing the complexity of culture. It is this uncritical view of culture that the liberation theologians suspect.

Incarnation differs from inculturation because it recognizes the unavoidably conflictual character of culture. Incarnation means that if the church models its approach to culture on the life of Christ, if it is "apostolic," it will not seek to diffuse itself equally through all the strata of society. Even less will it work principally with the most powerful elites. Rather, if the church practices discipleship as its form of inculturation (i.e., if it follows Christ into a culture as Christ entered his) then it will position itself, as he did, among the alienated and the rejected. It will incarnate itself with them, not as their tribune but as their friend and companion in struggle and in peace.

The critics of liberation theology, however, see this incarnational style as politicizing and divisive, or as a trend that reduces the universality of Christianity to a new kind of particularism. Why? Much of this debate has to do with the difference of opinion about the continuity between Jesus and his own Judaism. If we do not recognize the Jewishness of Jesus, then his own relationship to his culture becomes problematic. I have noticed, in reading the christological work of Cardinal Ratzinger and Leonardo Boff, that Ratzinger and his school, if we may call it that, insist that the church begins with the resurrection, *not* with the historical Jesus. They emphasize this because they believe that going back to the historical Jesus of the Gospels leads to a loss of the universal or eschatological significance of Jesus. Therefore they underline the complete break between the church and Israel, between the people of God in the New Testament and the Old Testament. This is the central point of Ratzinger's book *The New People of God* which, in effect, removes Jesus Christ from the culture in which he found himself and makes him a cultureless universal. The result, in my view, undercuts the whole idea of the incarnation. Consequently, it generates no guideline whatever for the proper relationship of the church to culture.

Liberation theologians also deal with the accusation that identification of the church with the poor, the same people with whom Jesus identified, ultimately leads to divisiveness and politicizing. But to reply to this we must first acknowledge a long-standing tendency of the church to legitimate poverty as a natural condition. How many times have we heard a prayer that goes something like this: "God, we thank you for the gospel, your church all around the world, which includes east and west, men and women, black and white, rich and poor. Amen." In prayers of this sort—and there are many—"rich and poor" are escalated into natural categories, part of the created world, like male and female, black and white. Such prayers supply a kind of "ontological" status to a condition that however is *not* natural but arises from human sin and injustice, which should *not* be equated with being male or female, black or white. This is a serious issue, because one sees in such prayers and in much of the literature critical of liberation theology an acceptance of the permanence of classes ("rich and poor") through all human history. The assumption is that there will always be privileged people and unprivileged people, rich and poor, top and bottom; to think of anything different is dismissed as "utopianism."

But can we allow economic injustice to be theologically legitimated by being celebrated as one of the natural and ontological differences God creates in a complex world? I think the answer is no. Poor and rich are not part of the natural diversity of the world. We should always try to make that clear. The church that exercises a preferential option for the poor is not opting for divisiveness but for faithfulness. It is seeking to be apostolic as the best way to be fully catholic.

# 8

# Rereading the Bible in Latin American Base Ecclesial Communities

## Pablo Richard

I work among peasants, young people, women, blacks, Indians, marginalized people—especially in El Salvador, Nicaragua, Costa Rica, and Panama with DEI (Departemento Ecumenico de Investigaciones), an ecumenical research center based in San Jose. The members of this center are the ones who are giving me my real doctorate in hermeneutics, in how to read the Bible. They are the focus of this reflection, and they are the subjects of this hermeneutic for liberation.

## THE BIBLE AS INSTRUMENT OF LIBERATION

The Latin American hermeneutic for liberation is rooted in the experience of God in the world of the poor. We call this *spirituality*. What is important in this spirituality is a political break with the dominant world, with the dominant structures and cultures of domination; this is a movement constructing a new world, the so-called popular poor peoples' movement. It is the world of the poor. But in this political break or reconstruction of society we have—and this is most important—a new experience of God. God is a different God. Here the break that we make is a break with idolatry. And here the enemy of faith is not atheism but idolatry. Normally all my friends who are atheists are *companions* in the struggle. I have no problems with the atheists. The atheists challenge us a lot. Our enemies are the idolaters. The problem is not unbelief in God; the problem is too many people that believe in God. Pinochet is a Roman Catholic, and Reagan is a mainline Protestant—that is the problem. The conquest of Latin America was done in the name of God. Slavery, in Latin America, was practiced by Christians. Current oppression continues to be caused by Christians. That is the problem: this perversion of the sense of God and image of God, this substitution of God by other gods (money, the market, prestige, power, and so on). We must break with idolatry and rediscover the presence of the God of Jesus Christ among the poor, the oppressed, the powerless. This new experience of God among the poor is the root of a new hermeneutical process.

Yet even though this experienced presence of the God of Jesus Christ among the oppressed is their most important experience, it is not sufficient as a *hermeneutic* of liberation. It is necessary to *discern* this presence of this God. This God is present among us, but God has a word. This God is present and speaking. God is not mute. Sometimes we have the image of a God who *spoke* to Abraham, who *spoke* in Jesus Christ, who *spoke* through the apostles, but who does not speak anymore. Today God is speaking. God speaks today as in the beginning of time, maybe even more. Therefore, if we believe that God is among the poor, it is necessary to *discern* her word, to *discern* her project, her will today, in very concrete situations. For instance, in Nicaragua, what is the will of God today? Or here in Boston, what is the will of God? What is the work of God, the project of God, for this society? The function of the church, the new historical subject, is to discern God's word, and therefore the church is prophetic. It is a prophetic community when this church is able to discern the word of God, when the church can say today in El Salvador the word of God, the will of God, the project of God here is that and that and that! Why say abstractions? Sometimes the church says, God's will is that we should all be good people. That does not make any sense. There is nothing prophetic in that. It is necessary to discern the word of God very concretely.

In order to do that we use the Bible. Just the Bible. It is the instrument to discern the word of God, the values of God. People use the Bible as an instrument, as a criterion of discernment. It is important to remember that the word of God is a reality that is greater than the Bible. The fathers of the church said that God wrote two Bibles. The first Bible is the facts of life, creation, history, women and men acting in history, and the second one is the text of the Bible. We must read the two Bibles. The church determined the canon, but that does not mean that God stopped speaking. No! God continues to speak.

The second thing to remember—and this may be shocking—is that the Bible is relative. What is absolute is the word of God. Sometimes we make the Bible an absolute. But the Bible is an instrument used to discern like a flashlight is used to light the path in the night. It is an instrument to discover the word of God. But when our poor people use the Bible to discern the word of God, when our communities, being prophetic communities, try to discern the word of God, they use the Bible as a relative instrument in order to discern what is absolute, the presence of God in our reality. They have to face a great problem: the Bible as it exists is not neutral. There is in the Bible a reading of the word of God that is very far from poor people. It is necessary to work in the Bible. The Bible is, in a certain sense, expropriated (alienated) from poor people. Therefore it is necessary to reappropriate it. There is a real struggle, a hermeneutical struggle. Therefore I avoid talking of a hermeneutical circle. It is rather a hermeneutical rupture, a hermeneutical break, a hermeneutical struggle.

In order to understand this struggle, it is important to establish some definitions. Here I will follow Carlos Mesters, a Brazilian exegete. To him, the Bible has three dimensions: (1) the text, (2) the history, and (3) the canon. Normally the structuralists, those who focus on literary analysis, insist on the text. The historicocritical method, the sociological reading of the Bible, insists a lot on the history of text, the past of the text, on the history in which the text was born. In Latin America today we insist on the canon.

What is canon? Canon is a measure. When the church established the canon it established a measure, a criterion to measure reality. It is like a meter. When I take a meter and I measure this wall, I can say, "This wall has twenty meters." The Bible has also this dimension. Not only the textual and the historical dimensions, but the Bible is also a canon with which to measure. It is a criterion to discern where God is, how God is, to discern her word; it is the grammar to articulate today the word of God. Therefore the Bible has not only a present and a past but also a future. The Bible has the force, and that is the sense of canon. Let us take Hebrews 4:12: "The word of God is living and active, sharper than any two-edged sword, piercing to the division of soul and spirit,

. . . discerning the thoughts and intentions of the heart." Also 1 Peter 1:23: "You have been born anew, not of perishable seed but of imperishable, through the living and abiding word of God." Or 1 Thess. 2:13: "the word of God, which is at work in you believers." The Bible is at work in us believers. This is the spiritual feature of the text.

The three dimensions are very important. It is interesting to compare these three dimensions in patristic thought. The early fathers spoke about the literal and the spiritual sense of the Bible. The literal is the historical sense. The spiritual is this dimension of the text as instrument, to work with; it discerns the word of God for a given society. It creates a new reading of the word of God. In this spiritual sense there are three approaches to the text: allegorical, topological, and analogical. The allegorical sense means that in the Bible we find a new understanding of faith. The topological, moral sense means that in it we find a new praxis. In the analogical sense, we find in the biblical text a new utopia. To the early fathers, in the Bible we have not only history, even though history is very important. But in it we have also an instrument to create in history a new understanding of faith, of praxis, of the future, the utopia, the eschatology.

## THE CLASH OF HERMENEUTICAL COMMITMENTS

What does this mean to our hermeneutical struggle? In the first place we discover that the Bible has been actually read by the dominant subject. And who is the dominant subject? He is the subject of the dominant system with all its dimensions: economical, political, social, cultural, ideological, spiritual, sexual, racial. This domination, normally, expresses itself through a certain model of the church that internalizes all these structures: the economical, the political, the spiritual structures of domination. Then we have a rich church, an authoritarian church, a church that is *male dominant,* a church that oppresses cultures and peoples. When this dominant subject reads the Bible, he perverts and distorts the Bible. The analysis of this biblical distortion is crucial for the understanding of the rereading of the Bible by the poor in Latin America.

The dominant subject destroys the Bible with two breaks; one is the break with the historical dimension, and the other is the break with the spiritual dimension of the Bible. Cut off from its historical dimension and cut off from its spiritual dimension, the text of the Bible becomes more and more an abstraction without history and without spirit. There is a historical and spiritual perversion of the text. The Bible receives a new historical context and a new consciousness: the historical context of the dominant system and the consciousness of the dominant class, the dominant culture, the dominant ideology—the dominant idolatry! The whole text is subjected to this new historical and spiritual context; a context of domination; a culture, an idolatry of domination. The following are a few examples of perversions of the text created by the hermeneutic of domination.

*Perversions in translation.* Translations are never simply translations; translations are always reconstructions. When the Bible is captive to a dominant reading, we face the great danger that a translation will make a reconstruction that produces the historical and spiritual situation of the dominant classes. Translations are continuously betraying the text. In this sense it is useful for the hermeneutical struggle to know also Hebrew and Greek. In translation, therefore, we have the first attempt of the dominant classes, the dominant cultural, ideological, and ecclesiastical systems to pervert the Bible.

*Perversion in the presentation.* The headings of the pericopes, the parallel selections, the notes, the whole presentation of the Bible, when the Bible is separated from its historical and spiritual roots, can function to distort the intention of the text.

*Semantic perversion.* Words in the text are perverted when their deeper meaning is distorted. The dominant system selects those texts that are more vulnerable, and after perverting these texts it uses them as the dominant discourse (the hermeneutical key) for the whole Bible. Here are some examples. "Blessed are the poor in spirit" (Matt. 5:3). If you pervert the word *spirit,* translating *spirit* as *soul* you end up saying, "Blessed are those who are poor in their soul." The whole sermon on the mountain, the whole gospel is perverted. Here is another example. "Render to Caesar the things that are Caesar's, and to God the things that are God's" (Mark 12:17). If you interpret Caesar as representing politics and God as the realm of the church, with this perversion you have the conclusion that faith and politics must be completely separated. The same happens in Matt. 10:28: "Do not fear those who kill the body but cannot kill the soul." If you understand soul as the dominant understand it, you are perverting its biblical meaning as that which gives life to our bodies, to our whole existence. Bishop Vega from Nicaragua said, "The contras kill only the bodies but the Sandinistas are killing the soul." (The Gospel said, "Do not fear those who kill the body.") So what Bishop Vega is saying is "Don't fear the *contras* . . . fear the Sandinistas."

*Ideological perversions.* First, there is the perversion of the inner structure of the text for instance, the translation of *sarx* and *pneuma* as body and soul. The real sense of *flesh* is the tendency to death, and the *spirit* is the tendency to life; it is the contradiction life/death that explains the opposite flesh/spirit. But when that is translated as body and soul, this profound distortion of these two elements provokes a whole distortion of the "whole" message of the New Testament and the Old Testament. Second, there is the distortion of the interlocutor. For example the commandment "You shall not steal" was given to the rich to protect the poor, but the ideological perversion makes of it a commandment given to the poor to protect the rich.

*Literary structural perversions.* Books that are very important become secondary (James and Philemon, for example, in the New Testament). There is also a perversion in the internal structure of books. Elisabeth Schüssler Fiorenza points to Mark 14, where there are two reports of the last supper. We usually speak of the second only as the last supper, and yet it is in the first text that Jesus is recognized as the Messiah by a woman, and Jesus himself said that because of her recognition of him she would be also recognized everywhere where the gospel was to be preached. But we never hear the gospel in memory of her in our churches. This is a perverted reading of the record. The inner structure of the text is perverted. In the Old Testament we have Abraham, Sarah, and Hagar. Normally, the text is read from the perspective of Abraham, but what if we read the text from the perspective of Hagar? It is a new text.

In Latin America we are rereading the Bible from the perspective of the poor and oppressed. We are trying to recover the historical dimension of the Bible as well as its spiritual dimension and to read the text in light of those dimensions. The roots of our hermeneutic are the spirituality of the poor and their experience of God in their situation because this is the only perspective from which they can argue about the word of God today. From this spiritual perspective we can recover the historical and spiritual dimensions of the text, and from this perspective we try to break with the dominant reading and its perversions.

All this is done in the base communities. The base communities are the locus where all this appropriation, expropriation, reappropriation, this reconquest, this destruction of the perversion that is in the text is done. The base communities are prophetic exactly because they are recovering the history hiding behind the text, the repressed memory of the poor and oppressed. They are the subject of this hermeneutic of liberation.

I believe that scientific exegesis is very important. But it is necessary to determine which is the trunk that supports, that gives life to the exegesis, and which are the roots of the actual exegesis. I suspect that sometimes the dominant exegesis only reproduces the perversions of the text. It is a reproduction of the dominant reading of the Bible. Sometimes I hear people saying, "The more I read the Bible, the less I understand the commentaries, and the more I read the commentaries, the less I understand the Bible." This is very tragic but very real. Sometimes the commentaries on the Bible talk about hundreds of issues but never about the word of God, the spiritual message of the gospel. It is necessary to maintain this level. Scientific exegesis is very much necessary today, maybe even more than before. But it is also necessary to ask which is the church where I make exegetical decisions and what are its roots. Sometimes there is a break between the level of exegesis and the base communities and the spirituality of the poor. At those times we are lost. It is necessary to reconstruct this level of scientific exegesis and to root out our exegesis in the spirituality of the poor. When we do that we really recover this third level, the most difficult, the last but also important conquest of the spirituality of the poor.

## References

Boff, Leonardo. 1985. *Church: Charism and Power: Liberartion Theology and the Institutional Church*. New York: Crossroad.

Fiorenza, Elisabeth Schüssler. 1983. *In Memory of Her*. New York: Crossroad.

Mesters, Carlos. 1984. *Defenseless Flower*. New York: Orbis Books.

# 9

# Christian Faith and Socialism: A Latin American Perspective

## Otto Maduro

There are three aspects of my biography that have profoundly influenced my theological beliefs. I am (1) a Latin American Catholic; (2) a sociologist of religion; and (3) one who identifies with democratic socialism as a way out of oppression. Democratic socialism indeed needs to be further examined and defined, but for the time being I might say that for me it points toward liberation. I will come back again to the theme of liberation, in relationship to North American theological concerns. First, however, I will explore the relationship of Marxism to the Roman Catholic Church, giving special attention to its Latin American context, where the social facts are now moving us toward a new understanding of the historical conflict between these two social forces.

North American readers are aware, of course, that there is and has been a conflict between Catholic religious beliefs and organizations, on the one hand, and Marxist theories and movements, on the other. This conflict has often been regarded by both Catholics and Marxists as the inevitable outcome of an *essential* incompatibility between religion and Marxism. As a Latin American Catholic democratic socialist, I question the essentiality of this incompatibility.

Does the sociology of religion have something new to say regarding this conflict? In Latin America the mutual concerns of many Christians and Marxists are moving us toward a new approach to this question and a new understanding of the history of the question itself.

One could say that for sociology there are no "essential" conflicts, but rather conflicts are the result of a rationalizing perception of each of the respective actors toward the other. For example, Catholics sometimes view Marxism as "intrinsically perverse," or Marxists look at religion as "the opiate of the people." These perceptions might acquire a certain autonomy in relation to their social origins, thus contributing to the deepening and reinforcing of the original conflict long after the conditions that gave rise to them have ceased to exist. Under different circumstances, however, an "ideological" conflict of this kind might begin to disappear, as when new social processes undermine the conflicting perception of these groups. Sometimes these new social processes might be hindered by the ideological conflict itself.

One interesting example of ideological interference is the nineteenth-century conflict between the church and the forces for democracy and trade unionism. For Pope Pius IX and for the church of his time, democracy and trade unionism were evil forces (Ihm 1981, 300, esp. no. 25). They were thought to be *intrinsically* atheist and harmful to Christianity and thus "essentially" incompatible with Catholic beliefs and organizations. By the turn of the century, under Pope Leo XIII, the perceived conflict was lessening, and it began to be thinkable for a Catholic to support democracy and trade unionism without having to renounce his or her faith (Ihm 1981, 241–61). One hundred years after Pius IX, under Pius XII, it became almost compulsory for a Catholic to vote Christian Democrat and to back Christian trade unions (Ihm 1981, 185).

What happened? Certainly, this was not merely a matter of theologicophilosophical change. The decline of the nobility as the ruling class together with the rise of the bourgeoisie and the proletariat made Pius IX's "political theology" outdated. Simultaneously, the need of the new ruling class for a certain religious legitimization of the new social order made the bourgeois atheism of the Enlightenment outdated. Thus the church and democracy met on new social grounds and theologicophilosophical transformations in both parties became imperative.

## THE CONFLICT BETWEEN CHRISTIANITY AND SOCIALISM

To understand better the conflict between the church and socialism we might pose some sociological questions. What were the social grounds of the original confrontation between the church and Marxist socialism? What were the social relations between these groups and the social classes linked with socialism?

In the nineteenth century the higher clergy of the Catholic church was closely linked to the ruling class of feudal society—the nobility. This identification between the church and the nobility was so deep that almost 100 percent of the French bishops in 1800 were feudal lords and nobles themselves. Quite naturally to them, the crisis of the feudal order with the rise of capitalism brought about a crisis for Catholicism, too. Both the nobility and the Catholic hierarchy strove to defend the other against the bourgeois menace, and atheism became one of the leading ideologies of the radical bourgeoisie. At the same time a new oppressed class—the proletariat—was born from what was left of peasants and artisans in the newly urbanized areas. The ideology of socialism emerged from among these proletarians.

Although most socialist groups were actually forced either to abandon the church or to give up their political ideals, the clash of socialism with Catholicism did not gain momentum before the end of the nineteenth century. Until then the nineteenth century's theologicopolitical stage was occupied by the struggle against liberalism. It was only after the church reconciled itself with the new elites and ceased acting as a serious threat to the new social order and after Marxism appeared to be gaining strength that the church's struggle against socialism became of major importance.

Marxist atheism requires an analogous sociological approach. Although communism and socialism were *religious* in their origins, the theological conditions of the last century as outlined above made it practically impossible for a political movement to remain simultaneously Christian and socialist for a long time. Actually, almost all of the Christian socialist organizations of the last century disappeared after a short time; their leaders, having been banned by the church, were forced to give up either their religion or their socialism or both.

Marx and Engels were socially bourgeois and intellectually formed in bourgeois atheism. The appeal of their atheism is both a symptom and a result of the nineteenth-century political impossibility of remaining both politically involved *and* indifferent toward religion. Not having the social and cultural means of remaining socialist within Christianity, many were forced to hold on to the anti-Christian bourgeois philosophy—atheism. This option, while constituting a handicap for the development of socialism during its first decades, proved to be an efficient way in which to keep socialism coherent and autonomously alive through subsequent years. As happened with Catholic anti-socialism, Marxist atheism acquired a significant autonomy in relation to its socioreligious origins, thus contributing to the reinforcement of the Catholic tradition of perceiving socialism as intrinsically atheist and therefore incompatible with the Christian faith.

## Changing Times

Since the beginning of World War I, many events have changed the nature of the conflict between the church and socialism, both within and outside the Catholic church. Among these is the development of the working class as a class-for-itself. Quantitatively as well as qualitatively, in many capitalist countries, the proletariat has grown as its consciousness, organizations, and struggles for power have developed throughout the past seven decades. Because of this emerging working class, Marxist socialism also grew—especially, lately, in the third world. Capitalism faces not only economic, political, and ecological crises but a crisis of credibility, as does Soviet Marxism.

Concomitantly the Catholic church has been undergoing major changes during this century. The social origins of its hierarchy as well as its social allegiances have experienced a gradual democratization. Consequently the focus of its pastoral work increasingly has been shifting from the elite to the peasantry, the proletariat and their children. But these social groups, having been influenced by bourgeois and socialist ideologies, have not resigned themselves to a merely passive role within the church. Their exigent presence has promoted consequential transformations of the official positions of the church, thus weakening the influence of the bourgeoisie.

No doubt secularization has played a significant role in the weakening of the bourgeois influence. Perhaps we can say that as the need of religious legitimization of the establishment decreases, the pressure of the ruling class upon the church diminishes along with the advantages received by the church. This allows a larger margin of action for religious organizations. Within this framework certain encyclicals (*Pacem in Terris* and *Populorum Progressio, Laborem Exercens* and *Sollicitudo Rei Socialis*, for instance), as well as certain declarations of Vatican II, acquire sound sociological meaning.

## The Latin American Context

Latin America is a vast continent of oppressed and believing people. Ninety percent Catholic, this continent has suffered for more than a century the ravages of industrial capitalism—economically, culturally, and ecologically. Under capitalist domination an accelerated process of forced migration and proletarianization has radically changed the situation of the peasantry. Socialist ideologies, Marxism among them, have found a fertile soil, mainly among our urban students, intellectuals, and industrial workers.

Both Catholic anticommunism and Marxist atheism were *imported* from Europe because of social problems in Latin America. From roughly 1920 to 1960, the traditional alliance of the church to white wealthy landowners served to strengthen a certain power and appeal of Marxist atheism. Marxist atheism, however, prevented democratic socialism from flowering into a viable alternative for the oppressed and believing masses of the continent. United in their common fear of communism, the liberal bourgeois parties, traditionally anticlerical, and the church's hierarchy finally came to terms in most Latin American countries, thus helping to consolidate capitalist domination of this continent—and a very undemocratic brand of capitalism in most cases, by the way.

Events of the sixties in Latin America, as in many other regions of the West, led to a period of reexamination of sociopolitical and religious assumptions. First, the successful Cuban revolution, despite its shortcomings, showed that socialism was not an impossible dream for the Latin American people. Immediately thereafter Marxist guerrillas spread all over the continent, striving unsuccessfully to convert workers and peasants to a socialist alternative. Second, in response to these Marxist efforts military and economic dependence on the United States was intensified in order to fight the guerrillas. Third, the widening gap between China and the USSR undermined not only socialist coalitions but also overseas dependence and its monolithic ideology, thus clearing the way for new, autonomous socialist approaches to Latin American problems.

Pope John XXIII, Vatican II, Pope Paul VI, and the new trends within European Catholic theology allowed fresh air to blow upon the Catholic intellectual milieu in Latin America as elsewhere. A certain criticism of capitalism and private property and of economic and political oppression of the poor began to become thinkable for Catholics, and Marxism was no longer necessarily considered diabolic, at least if it remained on a theoretical level. Many people, clergy and laity, particularly those living among the oppressed classes, felt they were no longer restrained from taking radical political action.

In this context, Camilo Torres, the Colombian priest and guerrilla, became a symbol and a challenge for the church of the sixties in Latin

America. Shortly after his death the Second Latin American Bishops' Conference (CELAM II) assembled in his country with Pope Paul VI. Although CELAM II (usually called "Medellín" after the conference site) condemned revolutionary violence as a means to achieve social justice and reiterated the theme of the incompatibility of Christianity with Marxism, it did constitute the first official step of the Latin American church to speak out against capitalistic oppression (Conference of Latin American Bishops 1970). With CELAM II the power of rather conservative Christian Democracy, already weakened by the translated works of Emmanuel Mounier, Teilhard de Chardin, and other more radical thinkers and by the failures of the Chilean and Venezuelan Christian Democratic experiments to offer an alternative to capitalism, faced the beginnings of its demise as the one and only political alternative for believing Catholics of the Left (Maduro 1987, 106–19).

Beginning in 1969 a growing number of Catholics (priests, nuns, and lay people) became involved in social work among the peasantry, in the urban slums, and in the factories of Latin America. The Catholic church's new, less conservative approach to social problems made it easier for the Catholic activists among the poor to understand, accompany, and support the political awakening of the oppressed.

This religious legitimization of the liberation struggles of the oppressed was totally new in Latin America, at least on the scale to which it has developed since the seventies. It provoked a chain reaction within and outside the church. This new attitude of the church stimulated a growing class consciousness, a movement toward local organization, and a political mobilization of the poor against economic and political oppression. Moreover, priests and nuns served as credible spokespersons before governments, press people, and international organizations. This made it more difficult for the police and the military to repress the struggles of the poor, to hide the oppression and the repression suffered by the latter, and to blame "communist atheists" for those struggles of the poor.

This process of legitimizing liberation struggles led immediately to pressure upon the church hierarchy to suppress the movement, thus stimulating the conflicts between conservative and progressive forces within the church itself. Although these pressures have not succeeded, there has been for the first time in Latin American history a systematic and growing hardening of the police and the military against the large progressive sector of the church. Every year more and more clergy people in more and more countries are imprisoned, expelled, tortured, and killed by the military. It is out of an effort to understand these recent events within a Christian perspective that a new theology, a theology of liberation, is emerging.

## A Theology of Liberation

In Christian base communities, in prisons, on demonstration lines, in factories, in hiding places, and in the slums Latin American Catholic groups and Marxist organizations have been meeting on new social grounds for more than two decades. Politically weaker than they were in the sixties and also less monolithic, more divided, and more independent, Marxists are experiencing a church other than "the opiate of the people" as Marx and Engels saw it. Catholics, theologically freer, less unanimous, and now gradually estranged from the ruling classes, are experiencing a Marxism that seems not to be "intrinsically perverse."

United in common this-world actions, growing numbers of Marxist and Catholic groups are compelled to question and overcome their traditional "essential incompatibility" stances. Thus a new Catholic approach to Marxism is being born within the church, while a new Marxist approach to religion, progressively disengaging from traditional dogmatic atheism and anticlericalism, is slowly spreading among the socialists. Both these new approaches seem to reinforce the other; hence new theoretical conditions have been allowed in some movements aiming toward a certain cooperation between Latin American Christian churches and Marxist political organizations.

Of course this process creates new conflicts, both within the church and within Marxism. In fact, a certain "institutional anomie" seems to be appearing on both sides. While the traditional politicoreligious dogmas crumble, many groups within both parties begin to lose their points of reference, resulting in a tendency for both to want to retain more rigid positions (the new or old ones). Probably because of its traditional allegiance with the ruling classes, the church experiences an inner reaction against the new "converging trend" regarding socialism, a reaction that does not seem to have a parallel in Marxist organizations— slower than the churches in recognizing both the novelty and the significance of this process. The partial reinforcement of the "conflicting trend" within the church shows itself, mainly in the hierarchy, as a recreance of centralism, authoritative rule, verticality, and dogmatism. Simultaneously, the majority of the Catholic hierarchy is led to support, overtly or silently, the apolitical (for example, the Charismatics), antipolitical, or decidedly right-wing (for example, Tradition, Family, and

Property, Opus Dei) Catholic groups, to the detriment of the "popular church," a term banned by Pope John Paul II.

What will be the outcome of this complex process? It is difficult to foretell, but a deeper sociological analysis of the past and present could help the church to understand its political role in today's capitalist society and help it to reexamine its allegiances to the upper classes. Our global future may well lie somewhere in this sociological task.

## A THEOLOGY OF LIBERATION FOR NORTH AMERICA

For North American oppressed groups a sociological analysis of the social structures, including the capitalist economic structure, within which they exist, could bring new light to their condition of marginalization and to the subsequent task of moving out into liberation. As a Latin American sociologist with a certain connection with North American theological concerns, I would like to add to the above analysis with a few remarks about this theology of liberation, beginning with what I think liberation theology in North America is often thought to be but is *not*.

First, Latin American liberation theology is not a theological justification of revolutionary violence, nor a rationalization of violence. To be sure the theology of liberation has arisen from within a deep comprehension of the social origins of revolutionary violence, origins that lie in the previous structural violence constituted by the oppression and repression of the many by the few, of the poor by the rich. Probably there were moments in some countries and in some groups in which some theologians of liberation rationalized revolutionary violence. But I must stress that liberation theology is *not* that—nor has it ever gone further than Thomas Aquinas in this respect. To reduce it to that is really to do violence to its realities. It is not to see the movement as it is developing. I would add that we Christians in Latin America today are learning a lot from North American and European pacificism.

Second, Latin American liberation theology is *not* a Marxist theology or a Christian justification or foundation of Marxism, although, indeed, within the theology of liberation there has arisen a new approach toward Marxism. Within this new approach, Marxism can be seen as a challenge for us Christians (1) to demonstrate practically that we are *not* the opiate of the people; (2) to understand better the importance of social analysis in the fight against social injustice; and (3) to appreciate the power of cooperation (along with its tensions and conflicts) of many groups fighting against oppression.

Third, Latin American liberation theology is *not* primarily an academic intellectual activity. When I hear some Afro-Latin musical pieces, especially their lyrics, I recognize a theology of liberation flowing. Often I find the words of these songs much more powerful than the words of an academic article, keynote address, or book. That is not to deny that professional theologians and the university have often played a significant role in the development of this theology. I would say that they have been the intellectual chroniclers and articulators of processes that were already going on or about to erupt. They have also been on the side of processes taking place at the base of society; thus the theological, academic, and intellectual elites have been hindered in their counter reaction to this movement developing within the people.

Finally, Latin American liberation theology is *not* one more system of thought. It is not a new doctrine, a new ideology, or a new list of theological propositions that one ought to accept or to which one ought to assent in order to be saved. Latin American liberation theology as a movement does not preclude the need for partial provisory systemizations of theological reflection. Rather it explicitly or implicitly considers them partial and provisory, merely something to be constantly reassessed and redone.

What then is theology of liberation? It is a new mode of theologizing, a new way of doing theology that goes back to the oldest one in the Judeo-Christian tradition. It is new for us but not new in human history. It is a mode of theologizing that is more communitarian than individual. It arises somewhat spontaneously from within Christian base communities, from within the poor, from within the processes of oppression and awareness, from the struggles of the poor for liberation, from their struggles against repression, from their organizations, from their reflection on all of these dimensions of their lives under the light of Christian faith. It is a new mode of theologizing in which the subjects are the oppressed and believing lay people. They are no longer the mere objects of theologizing but the very subjects of this new way of doing theology.

Liberation theology is a new mode of theologizing where the context and theological perspective are that of oppression and liberation; where the intention is not that of theoretical orthodoxy but that of helping one another on the path of spiritual and, therefore, material liberation.

If there is one key dimension to Latin American liberation theology, it is that we are unable to understand spiritual salvation as separated from or taking place independently of material, social, political, and economic liberation. In this sense, theology of liberation is a movement, not merely an intellectual movement but a vital cultural movement implying not only theology *strictly speaking,* but also the music, poetry, dancing, and prayer of liberation.

Liberation theology is a *new* mode of theologizing because, although the thrust is the oldest in Judeo-Christianity, the vantage point has changed *back* to those for whom, from whom, and among whom Jesus lived and spoke.

## References

Conference of Latin American Bishops (CELAM II). 1970. *The Church in the Present-day Transformation of Latin America in Light of the Church Council.* Bogotá: General Secretariat of CELAM.

John Paul II. 1983. Homily. Reprinted in *National Catholic Reporter* (March 18).

Ihm, Claudia Carlen, ed. 1981. *The Papal Encyclicals 1740–1887.* New York: McGrath Publishing. Rerum Novarum by Leo XIII, 241–61; Nostris et Nobiscum, 292–303, and Quanta Cura, 381–86, by Pius IX.

Maduro, Otto. 1987. Christian Democracy and the liberating option for the oppressed in Latin America. *Concilium* 193.

———. Labor and religion according to Karl Marx. *Concilium* 131.

Pius XII. 1948. His Excellency. *The Tablet* 191 (May 1).

———. 1948. Una ben intima. *The Tablet* 191 (March 20).

# 10

# The Character of Liberation Ethics

## Peter J. Paris

———

Liberation thought has been associated primarily with the rise of a new form of theological understanding that for nearly two decades has waged wholesale, frontal attacks on the Western theological tradition. Although the various liberation theologies (e.g., Latin American, black American, feminist, etc.) share common elements, chief among them all is their vigorous denial that theology can ever be culturally transcendent and epistemologically universal. Rather, liberationists argue that sociopolitical values inhere in the basic presuppositions underlying all theologies. More specifically, they argue that the basic presuppositions underlying the Western theological tradition reveal the latter's solidarity with the basic societal values of their ruling elites. The established church traditions of Western Europe, the pervasive nature of the Protestant ethos in America, and the fact that theology has been for centuries a white male preserve constitute significant loci for gathering evidence supportive of the liberationists' argument that the Western theological tradition constitutes a basic paradigm of cultural infusion.

Thus for these and other reasons liberation theologies condemn the entire Western theological enterprise on the grounds that the latter's understanding of God has been conditioned by its social location, which by definition has always stood in opposition to the struggles of oppressed peoples for liberation. Hence, the most fundamental claim made by all liberation theologies is their radically different understanding of the nature and activity of God, that is, for example, their bold proclamation that God's activity in history is solely that of being in solidarity for liberation with the specific struggles of oppressed peoples. In fact God is characterized as the God of the oppressed, and the biblical sources are carefully mined for verifying evidence relative to the truth of this claim. For many liberationists the Exodus tradition has gained a position of primacy among theological symbols because it explicitly sets forth God's liberating activity in relation to an oppressed people. Further they view the various biblical pericopes depicting God's solidarity with the poor and the disinherited as continuous with the symbolic power of the Exodus event. Many feminists, however, in their struggle against the patriarchalism in the Bible, have sought to uncover concealed traditions in the record that speak more specifically to women's experience than the Exodus event does.

In summary liberation theologies agree on the following. The mainline Catholic and Protestant theologians in the West have betrayed the Christian gospel by depicting God in their own image, evidenced by their use of such anthropomorphic symbols as *Ruler, Victor, Lord,* and the like. Contrary to the Western theological tradition, liberation theologies view themselves collectively as a prophetic movement bent on cleansing the Christian tradition by restoring the image of God as one who is in solidarity with the liberation struggles of oppressed peoples, thus affording the latter a place of hermeneutical privilege.

The prophetic aim of liberation theologies is for ecclesiastical change both in thought and action. Clearly every such prophetic event provokes a conflict between the established theologies and the prophetic challenge. The latter is almost always resisted vigorously by the former, usually through attempts to discredit it as false, blasphemous, selfserving, and destructive of peace and unity. Such declarations can easily provide justification for the use of more coercive means of ridding theology of such an unwelcome intruder. Sometimes the prophetic challenge may be effectively marginalized by bestowing on it a measure of legitimacy, thus dissipating the force of the challenge. Such appears to be the present status of liberation theology in our divinity schools and theological seminaries.

By definition, each genre of liberation theology provides theological justification for some particular liberation struggle. In fact, each liberation theology claims not only to have emerged out of some liberation movement but to have as its goal the enhancement of that struggle. In other words, liberation theologies view themselves as practical throughout—praxis designating its origin, agency, form, and end. As mentioned above, liberation theologies argue that every theology is political in a similar way; none is transcendent of its sociopolitical context. Rather, each reflects some basic set of beliefs, convictions, or values that are presupposed at the point of departure and that condition the entire enterprise from beginning to end.

Note that these presupposed beliefs, convictions, and values designate the fundamental commitments of their adherents and are always viewed by the latter as commensurate with their religious faith. These presuppositions are starting points and, as such, are not demonstrated truths. That is to say, they did not become convictions by rational argument. Rather, they are given by experience; they constitute the content of character formation. We do not mean to imply that they are irrational. On the contrary, they can become the subject of rational inquiry at any time for the sake of gaining conceptual clarity about their nature. But convictions of this kind are not established by such a procedure.

Our daily experience is replete with examples of these convictions. The 1986 confirmation hearings for the chief justice of the Supreme Court centered around the issue of personal conviction: "Is Rehnquist or is he not extremist in his beliefs about individual rights, the equality of blacks and women, the relation of government and religion? If so, can he rightly and justly lead the Supreme Court?" Similarly, when the U.S. government repeatedly refused to negotiate with the Palestine Liberation Organization (P.L.O.) until the latter acknowledged Israel's right to exist, it (the U.S. government) was, in fact, pressing the issue of convictions that it rightly believed would condition all aspects of the negotiating process. Correspondingly, the once constant demand of the South African government that Nelson Mandela and the African Nationalist Congress (A.N.C.) renounce their commitment to violence as a condition for negotiation also centered on the conflict over contrary convictions. In each case, an adequate and sufficient response would have constituted a simple affirmative statement, not an argument.

Clearly, the nature of one's convictions sets the frame of reference for all of one's thinking and action. Liberation theologies argue that these basic convictions make all the difference and that they arise out of one's sociopolitical experience. These convictions not only constitute beginning points but they designate final ends. They are rightly the subject matter of theological and philosophical analysis.

## ISSUES FOR LIBERATION ETHICS

During the past two decades liberation theology has done more than any other discipline to give the plight and activity of the oppressed maximum visibility in the classrooms of academe and the consciences of the churches. This in itself has been a significant contribution to social ethics. But liberation thought presents many more moral issues that need the careful attention of social ethicists. We should note that in order for such ethical inquiry to be commensurate with liberation thought it must make the practical task of liberating oppressed peoples its subject matter. Thus, unlike traditional ethics, the goal of such inquiry would not be systematic theory but improved praxis. In this sense, thought and action are not only integrally related but the one is for the sake of the other (i.e., thought is for the sake of action).

The sources that determine the character of the liberation theologies are experience, Scripture, revelation, and tradition—all of which are viewed as interrelated; hence, they are not ranked in any order of primacy. Clearly, experience is very important to liberation thought even as it is to any thought. But in the liberation motif experience refers to that of the oppressed and, consequently, draws widely on all rational means available for describing it. This includes the resources of the social sciences, literature, history, art, and so on. In short, this source designates the necessity of an interdisciplinary method. Its view of the commensurability of reason with revelation, Scripture, and ecclesiastical tradition is similar to the Catholic tradition and, consequently, helpful to ethical inquiry since the latter need not be required to set forth any special apology concerning the function of reason, as is frequently the case in protestant Christian ethics. All liberation thought has a positive view of reason. Its fundamental quarrel with much of Western scholarship lies with the latter's attempts to conceal the way in which social location constitutes a necessary conditioning factor on reason. In short, liberationists deny the possibility of pure reason.

Let us now consider some of the major ethical issues facing the ethicist committed to the liberationist project of liberating the oppressed.

*Descriptive analysis.* Much of the ethical analysis in liberation thought has been in the descriptive mode: often introducing moral data that have not been available hitherto either because they were unknown, deliberately ignored, or concealed. Since liberation thought takes as its point of departure some condition of oppression, adequate analysis of that oppression is of the utmost importance. Since every analysis implies a certain ethical orientation, both the analysis and its moral implications necessitate the most careful scrutiny. Carol Robb illustrates this clearly in her description of divergent feminist sociopolitical theories governing differing analyses of women's oppression (Robb 1981, 48–68). The *radical feminist* perspective views men and their inherent need for control as the root of women's oppression. *Sex-rolism* absolves men from all but psychological responsibility for the oppression of women. *Marxist-Leninist feminism* views women's oppression as a part of the class struggle against private ownership of property, which is considered the primary condition of social alienation. A *modified socialist feminism* tries to maintain feminist movement within the socialist collectivist struggle without becoming subsumed by the latter. The importance of Robb's analysis lies not only in her clear presentation of the different understandings of women's oppression but in how moral, social, and political values take on new meanings when they are defined in relation to different theories of oppression that are often implicit if not explicit in the work of feminist ethicists. Nevertheless, Robb concludes that feminists are in complete agreement about the fundamental ethical principles. "Self-determination for women, autonomy, and an inviolable sense of embodiedness figure prominently in all feminist visions of a new social order" (Robb 1981, 63).

Similarly, the condition of racism has been understood in divergent ways as well, and each such theory implies different ethical values relative to social justice. The *separatist tradition,* advocated in recent decades by Malcolm X and Albert Cleage, views whites as incurably racist and calls upon blacks to establish an alternative nation as the only means of liberation. The *integrationist tradition,* embodied in Martin Luther King, Jr., and strongly affirmed by James H. Cone, J. Deotis Roberts, and others, views whites as victims of a dilemma that takes the form of a self-contradiction between their most cherished beliefs, on the one hand, and their practices, on the other hand; this is nevertheless correctable by the moral agency of blacks (supported by others) whose task is to redeem the nation and the Christian faith. A *neosocialist* perspective (whose most recent representative is Cornel West) strives to combine a racial and class analysis in such a way as to do justice to both while avoiding the traditional tendency of reducing the one to the other. As with feminist social analysis the basic ethical principles inhere in the sociopolitical theory that explains the condition of oppression. Descriptive ethics clarifies the values implicit in both the social science and in the ethics. But, further, descriptive ethics can explicate significant hermeneutical principles functioning implicitly in social contexts and, if brought to clarity, serve to empower the struggle of liberation (Paris 1985).

*Critique of ethics.* Another important ethical dimension of liberation thought pertains to the critical analysis of the discipline of ethics itself in order to discern the ways in which it has served either implicitly or explicitly the values of the dominant sociopolitical elites. Valerie S. Goldstein and Barbara H. Andolsen have raised serious questions about the centrality of *agape* in Protestant ethics (especially the ethics of Anders Nygren, Reinhold Niebuhr, and Gene Outka) because it reflects male experience and ignores women's experience. More specifically, they argue that men stress "other regardedness" as more virtuous than their own excessive view of self-worth and, consequently, view women as being more virtuous because of their self-sacrificing spirit in the family, which renounces self-regard and results in very low self-esteem (Andolsen 1981). These feminists argue for the importance of mutuality as a relational ethic that they feel does more justice not only to women's experience but to women's self-esteem as well.

Similarly, Herbert O. Edwards argues that Reinhold Niebuhr's emphasis on Christian realism led him to advocate patience on the part of the "Negroes" since their demands for justice must yield to other facts. In other words, Niebuhr's emphasis on "taking all the facts into account" served as an apology for giving full support to the civil rights struggle in principle but taking it away in actual situations of moral conflict (Edwards 1986, 8–10).

*Conflicts among oppressed groups.* Sometimes one encounters two or more oppressed groups making contrary claims about the nature of God, the form of the social good, the content of moral and civic virtue, and the just distribution of economic and social resources. Then one is confronted with problems and dilemmas that require maximum ingenuity in ethical evaluation. There is no better illustration of this dilemma than the respective self-understandings and corresponding theologies of the Afrikaner and black Africans in South Africa. Both claim the experience of oppression as a primary condition governing their respective orientations to the world. Both claim that God is on their side of the struggle. Which is right? Both view themselves as special emissaries imbued with a sacred mission, and each views the other as the primary threat to its own well-being. Which is true? Both demand a radically different societal state. Which is more just? Clearly, such problems cannot be resolved solely by appeal to the theological thought of either group. A similar problem presents itself whenever one has two oppressed minorities in a circumscribed situation competing for scarce resources. The conflicts that exist between Hispanic and black

American groups in many of our major urban centers illustrates this issue.

*Improving relations among oppressed groups.* Another ethical problem facing liberation thought is how oppressed groups ought to relate to one another. Clearly they all possess loyalties to members within their own respective groups, but what is or ought to be the nature of their loyalty to other oppressed groups? Once again the ethicist is called upon to establish criteria that enable the expansion of moral community by enhancing the well-being of all concerned. This, I contend, is a political task that is never resolved once and for all. Rather, improved mutuality between and among groups necessitates continuous negotiation, the exact outcome of which is never predictable. Nevertheless, effective structures and relevant guidelines for such negotiations are essential and must be devised, advocated, and implemented.

*Violence vs. nonviolence.* One cannot discuss the ethical issues pertaining to liberation thought and overlook the question of violence vs. nonviolence. Moral arguments exist on both sides. Mahatma Gandhi, Martin Luther King, Jr., and Bishop Tutu represent three major public figures who condemn the use of violence; others feel obliged to advocate it only as a last resort. The latter tend to draw upon the just war tradition for ethical criteria justifying their position. But every ethicist must work out a position on this issue because of its centrality in determining the form of the liberation struggle.

*The primacy of justice as a teleological principle.* Here the basic telos of humanity is not abstracted from the historical situation as an ideal form. Rather, right societal forms constitute the telos we advocate. Liberation thinkers argue that oppressed groups seek primarily the affirmation of their humanity by the oppressors. They seek that which has been denied them, namely, equality with all other humans, which implies self-determination (the right to shape their own destiny). In short, black Americans, women, the poor, black South Africans, and all other oppressed groups seek their own well-being as self-determining people. The specific content of that search will vary from group to group and from context to context. But given that desired telos, all ethical questions pertain to the appropriate moral means for its realization. In this respect, ethics is determined by the end and hence is teleological. But this does not imply any turn away from the insights of other ethical traditions. It simply establishes a guide for their use.

For example, Beverly Harrison's argument for women's choice draws heavily on the tradition of rights and rules after establishing her desired end: woman as self-determining moral agent (Harrison 1983). Similarly, the contributions of contexturalists, relationists, virtue and value theorists are relevant. In brief, the entire ethical enterprise must be guided by the overriding telos, namely, the transformation of the oppressed into self-determining human beings.

## References

Andolsen, Barbara Hilkert. 1981. Agape in feminist ethics. *Journal of Religious Ethics* 9, no. 1 (September).

Edwards, Herbert O. 1986. Niebuhr, "realism," and civil rights in America. *Christianity and Crisis* 46, no. 1 (February 3).

Harrison, Beverly Wildung. 1983. *Our Right to Choose: Toward a New Ethic of Abortion.* Boston: Beacon Press.

Paris, Peter J. 1985. *The Social Teaching of the Black Churches.* Philadelphia: Fortress Press.

Robb, Carol S. 1981. A framework for feminist ethics. *Journal of Religious Ethics* 9, no. 1 (September).

Roman Catholic Bishops. 1980. *Origins, N C Documentary Service* 14 (November 15).

# 11

# Theologies of Liberation in Women's Literature

## Lorine M. Getz

Literature often reveals theological truth in story form that is otherwise overlooked because it is less accessible in more conventional modes of theological inquiry. In reading closely three women's liberation stories proceeding from three different racial and ethnic communities in the Americas—Anglo, black, and Hispanic—I have discovered that they hold helpful keys to furthering theological dialogue among these diverse cultural groups. Certainly, on the basis of an analysis of three works, I cannot make a definitive argument for inherent theological impediments to all American women's cross-cultural dialogue. Rather, I suggest that the evidence found in these three stories is sufficient to warrant a more thorough search of such liberation literature to determine if these differences are accidental to these stories or systemic to their respective cultures.

The method I will employ is an argument by analogy from literary device to theological concept. I am interested in how three stories (*The Women's Room* by Marilyn French, *Their Eyes Were Watching God* by Zora Neale Hurston, and *The House of the Spirits* by Isabel Allende) portray in literary form the range of theological understandings of the relation between nature and grace. This range encompasses traditionally defined schools of thought on the topic and sheds new light on feminist liberation conversations. This method is set forth in greater detail in my *Nature and Grace in Flannery O'Connor's Fiction* (1982).

I believe both the method and the theological insights from my earlier study are applicable here, since like the O'Connor corpus, the

141

women's liberation literature selected here is based on a Christian understanding of human experience and expressed in exacting literary form. The uniqueness of the O'Connor material helped me see clearly the possibilities of analogically pairing types of literary usage with understandings of experiences of liberation. In particular O'Connor, unlike the authors that will be discussed here, was not interested in expressing a single set of human experiences or any one particular quest. Rather she was a phenomenologist of the human condition and regularly experimented in depicting the full range of human/divine interactions, especially as related to questions of freedom and redemption. The examples of women's liberation materials selected here each proceed from a more restricted field of experience and articulate one specific set of ways in which the divine and the human are seen to interact around the concern of personal and societal liberation.

## LITERARY DEVICES

Like O'Connor, the writers I shall discuss employ specific literary devices to depict the action of liberating grace. Three devices that, when analyzed, reveal the dynamics of the divine/human interaction in which we have interest are *symbolization, discrepancy in action between intention and outcome,* and *moment of recognition.* As will be demonstrated, each of these devices can be utilized in several ways. When the three are paired together and employed in the same manner within a narrative, they can be said to portray a specific and distinctive type of grace-event (see Getz 1982, 24–32).

### Symbolization

In literature the depiction of the moment of grace described by O'Connor and the experience of liberation portrayed by the authors I shall examine here are obtained through the employment of multivalent symbols, that is, through the use of objects having clear and definite meaning on one level/dimension yet also meaningful in another sense and/or on another level/dimension within the narrative. It is at the moment of grace or freedom that the symbol changes or expands in meaning, becoming multivalent.

In some O'Connor stories, symbols may carry single, limited meanings, yet gradually attain other related and implied meanings, deepening and expanding the original connotation of the symbol. This multitude of additional meanings may include contradictions. But in the central moment of divine/human interaction, the protagonist sees the unexpected convergence of opposites, gains insight into the meaning of the symbol in all its various manifestations, and experiences the revelation of the full meaning of the symbol.

In this type of symbolism the original sense of the symbol is extended and gains significance previously unsuspected by either the protagonist or the reader. This additional meaning points beyond the original natural sense of the symbol to a new supernatural significance. The natural meaning of the symbol is retained and complemented by a further, supernatural meaning. Yet the unity of the meanings that make the symbol multivalent are confirmed at the moment of encounter. Grace entails the multivalent meanings of the natural and supernatural at one and the same time, enhancing and enriching the original meaning of a symbol.

In other O'Connor stories, grace functions in the resolution of a symbol by revealing its contradiction, that is, by showing that its natural meaning stands in opposition to its supernatural meaning. In such stories the reader recognizes the opposite meanings the symbol possesses, yet the protagonist is only aware of the natural meaning. Grace intervenes, discloses the true supernatural meaning of the symbol to the protagonist and presses either the acceptance of the symbol's newly revealed reality or its rejection. The act of liberation here centers in the enlightenment of the protagonist brought about by the tension between the two connotations of the symbol.

The first type of divine/human interaction employs symbols to indicate the complementary relationship between nature and grace through the enriching of the symbol. The second type begins with a multivalent symbol that expresses the conflict between nature and grace in the opposition between its natural and supernatural meaning. Through the action of grace, the supernatural element is upheld and confirmed as the real value.

Grace may also be depicted in yet a third way in multivalent symbols. Here the symbol becomes the active transformative principle in the liberating event. A symbol whose natural meaning is known to both the reader and the protagonist gradually takes on a supernatural meaning for the reader. The protagonist, who undergoes a radical change through the action of the symbol itself, gradually becomes transformed until she or he becomes identified with the new meaning of the symbol, while loosing her or his personal qualities through a process of metamorphosis. The void created in the loss of the protagonist's human nature is replaced by the transferred supernature, changing the identity of the protagonist, as grace displaces or transubstantiates nature. Here natural meaning is not enriched or reversed but displaced by a related, yet more intense supernatural meaning.

## Discrepancy in Action between Intention and Outcome

Grace can also be depicted in the use of a second literary device, namely, discrepancy in action between intention and outcome. The divine intervenes in the intended course of human action, uplifting, reversing, or impeding through its supernatural interference. When divine intervention facilitates the human intention, the goal of the protagonist is reached, yet it is also enhanced and ennobled. Continuity is maintained between the original intention and the final product, but the reader is aware of the discrepancy in that the final product transcends the capabilities of the protagonist. In other stories, the final product stands in opposition to the natural object of the human intentions, being thwarted and manipulated by the divine in order to reach a new, and opposite, supernatural goal. And finally divine intervention may be represented by the complete stopping or cessation of the action but not until the action has been driven beyond the intention of the protagonist. As the story develops, the action gains a momentum beyond her or his intention and control. When the action finally ceases, the protagonist has been victimized. She or he is completely incapacitated, totally displaced by grace. Now reduced to nonaction, the protagonist becomes a burnt-out case, a sign for others of the power of God.

## Moment of Recognition

A third way grace may be portrayed in literature is through recognition on the part of the protagonist that she or he possesses qualities and gifts that, though unmerited and unexpected, uplift or ennoble her or him. These gifts are seen as extensions of human nature, standing not in opposition but rather lending positive value to one's actions, value that is not derived from the nature of the action itself. In these stories the recognition of grace is presented as a maturation that develops from the positive aspects of human nature and builds on the integrity of a person's acting and willing. The divine action enriches and uplifts the natural condition, and the protagonist matures spiritually by gaining a broader understanding of divine providence in her or his life.

The protagonist may also recognize grace, in a quite different way, through being forced by some violent occurrence to a boundary situation. Recognizing her or his helplessness in the face of supernatural power, she or he now experiences the negation of the world structure or of human volition in the face of this supernatural meaning or action. The moment of recognition now constitutes the very disruption of her or his understanding of the natural situation, exposes the sin and error of the protagonist, and opens up the possibility of conversion as the protagonist recognizes this disruption to be the result of God's intervention.

The third use of recognition is characterized by the displacement of the protagonist through the action of grace so as to make any recognition impossible. In these stories the protagonist is not converted but broken and destroyed. In this type of grace-event, a secondary character, often the antagonist, recognizes the event as liberating. The secondary character sees in the destruction of the protagonist an act of God.

The responses of the protagonists vary. They may accept the call and change their lives radically, they may be inadequate to the revelation, or they may die as a result of it. It is only from the viewpoint of the reader that the full meaning of the protagonist's experience can be interpreted.

## THEOLOGICAL TYPES

I have just described three different ways that literary devices can be used in narratives to depict liberating events that can be seen as analogous to certain Christian doctrines of grace. These three representations are analogous to three systematic approaches to grace attributed respectively to the Thomistic, Augustinian, and Jansenistic schools.

### Thomism

The relationship between grace and nature generally attributed to the Thomistic school views divine intervention as building upon nature in a harmonious manner. Through the use of symbols in these kinds of stories, the natural meaning of the symbol is not negated in the resolution of the plot but is confirmed and expanded. As the narrative unfolds, the symbol gains an additional meaning beyond the natural capacities of the object that symbolizes it. This further meaning ennobles and uplifts nature. Within the symbol, grace completes nature.

The use of the literary device of discrepancy in action between intention and outcome here is such that the original human intention is confirmed and enhanced by the operation of grace. More than was expected in the natural order is given in the outcome of the act. This enhancement of nature is the effect of supernatural grace. Similarly, the moment of recognition that obtains in these stories results in a broader understanding by the protagonist of the fullness of God's love.

The common element in this first theological type is that grace builds on nature, adding a qualitatively new dimension to the natural order that is not owed to it, that is totally gratuitous, but that is not in opposition to or a negation of the natural elements.

## Augustinianism

The second or Augustinian view of grace has analogues to the use of the multivalent symbol involving the separation and rejection of the natural meaning of the symbol. The natural and supernatural meanings of the symbols are polarized, and the opposition between them is emphasized such that, in the moment of grace, the natural meaning is shown to belong to the order of sin. Similarly, in this use of discrepancy between intent and outcome, grace operates to reverse the original, natural intention of the protagonist. The outcome is not merely different from what the protagonist had intended, but the divine intention is actually contrary to the original goal. Moreover, the moment of recognition involves a call to repentance or conversion, an acknowledgment that the prior aspirations were in opposition to God's will.

According to this understanding of grace, the only right love is love for God. All other loves—familial, sexual, cultural—are sinful tendencies of the human heart that strive against grace. Augustinianism stresses the medicinal aspects of grace and the correlative disorder of human nature, which is in dire need of a cure. In order to save or liberate, grace must reverse the sinful tendencies that would otherwise lead humankind to damnation. This stress on the opposition between nature and grace, even though the ultimate purpose is reconciliation and salvation, is the point of analogy to the second use of literary devices in literature.

## Jansenism

The third type of grace differs significantly from the other two narrative forms in that the natural level is altogether displaced by the supernatural. The first mode, analogous to Thomism, is characterized by harmonious reconciliation of the symbolic meanings, by an enhancement of the protagonist's original intention, and by a recognition of this enrichment resulting in spiritual maturation. The second, analogous to Augustinianism, is distinguished by a separation and opposition of the levels of symbolic meaning, a reversal of the protagonist's intention, and the recognition of a call to conversion. Stories of this third type are characterized by a total displacement of nature by supernature.

In this type of narrative the natural meaning of the symbols is eliminated in favor of a supernatural meaning. Here the discrepancy in action is such that the natural plot development stops. The action of grace intervenes not merely to reverse the natural development of the story but to displace it completely. There can be no continuation of the narrative, since the protagonist has been burnt-out, transubstantiated by the action of grace. And there is no primary recognition or conversion, since the protagonist is no longer able to recall her or his former state. There is no continuity of selfhood. Following the action of grace, the protagonist is merely a sign of God's power. These characteristics suggest an analogy to Jansenism.

The key notion in Jansenism is that of irresistible grace. According to this understanding, nature is so corrupted by sin that, not only is grace necessary for redemption, but this grace must be so strong that in a fallen state one cannot resist it. Predestination is absolute. There is no such thing as grace offered and rejected, since grace, once offered, is overwhelming and must be accepted. Before the intervention of liberating grace, the natural and supernatural, material and spiritual levels were thoroughly antagonistic to each other. The former, sinful state is eliminated through the suffering of the victim, which works in conjunction with the operation of divine grace.

## THE WOMEN'S STORIES OF LIBERATION

The three stories I will discuss here—French's *The Women's Room*, Hurston's *Their Eyes Were Watching God,* and Allende's *The House of the Spirits*—emerged from different racial and ethnic settings. By the very fact that each has been published and made available in the male-dominated first world market, one could argue that they are the literary works of women who have "made it" in that world, that they do not adequately represent the oppressed, and that they are therefore themselves classist. I would argue that in each of the cultures represented by these works, women are oppressed because of their gender, and on that basis, as well as perhaps on others, these women legitimately seek liberation. Each, however, uses the literary devices described above to express a theology of liberation different from that of the others.

The problems of solidarity among women of different races and cultures are made significantly more complex by the gender issue, which is generally not addressed in liberation theologies other than by feminism. Not all of the authors I discuss are feminists in the traditional sense. This is partly because feminism has been thought of, often rightly so, as a white middle-class movement. French speaks as a white feminist; Hurston as a "Womanist," that is, as a black woman seeking liberation both as a woman and as a black; and Allende as an Hispanic liberationist woman.

Though the commonality of females seeking liberation in oppressive societies seems to some such an obvious reason to bond that solidarity among women should come swiftly, articulated cultural and unspoken theological issues present obstacles to their dialogue. I point to these barriers, at least in part, by bringing to light fundamental theological differences that must be addressed before one can hope to establish solidarity.

## *The Women's Room:*
## Thomistic Presentation of Liberation

In Thomistic fashion, French employs the three literary devices of symbolization, discrepancy in action, and moment of recognition to suggest that the liberation of white middle-class women is in harmony with their natural selves, follows a continuity with their true identities, and reaches a maturation previously unattainable to them. Thus, liberating grace complements women's nature.

### *Symbolization*

The symbol of "room" (in both the sense of a place and of a space) functions throughout the novel to develop the theme of woman's true place in society and the intrinsic worth of females in their own right. In the opening scene the central character, Mira Ward, whose husband of many years has recently divorced her, is huddling for safety in a basement ladies rest room at Harvard University. *Ladies'* has been scratched out and replaced by a scratched-in *Women's* on the outside of the door. As the novel progresses, that crude write-over signals Mira's growth from a respectable thirty-eight-year-old wife with tinted hair (the lady) to a mature woman in her own right (a liberated woman).

As the book opens, Mira sits fully clothed on the edge of an open toilet seat, feeling helpless and inadequate. Her thoughts are those of a female whose values revolve around a man and who is accustomed to being relegated to the basement of life:

> It would all have been redeemed, even translated into excitement, had there been some grim-faced Walter Matthau in a trench coat, his hand in a gun-swollen pocket, or some wild-eyed Anthony Perkins in a turtleneck, his itching strangler's hands clenching and unclenching—someone glamorous and terrifying at any rate—waiting for her outside in the hall. . . . She could have transcended, knowing she had one of them at home, and could therefore move alone in a crowd. (French [1977] 1986, 7–8)

The stall walls of the washroom are filled with random graffiti—SDS, Kill Pigs, Power to the People, Bread and Roses. On the blood red enamel wall behind her: Some Deaths Take Forever. The room itself was an afterthought in an out-of-the-way place in a building designed for men. Though this place of necessity for women had finally been added, there were, Mira knew, still other rooms in the building, not just the more convenient male rest rooms, from which she was restricted because of her gender.

As the novel develops, Mira begins to reflect on how in her former husband's house she had no room. Between his demands and those of her two sons, she had no private space, no room of her own. Her life, from pregnancy on, she realizes, was owned by another creature; she was literally a "ward" as she still calls herself. To reinforce her theme, French cites Virginia Woolf: "Haven't they [Women], throughout time, worked as hard as men, labored in vineyard and kitchen, in field and house? How is it the men ended up with all the pounds and pence? Why do women not even have a room of their own, when in her day, at least, every gentleman had his study?" (French [1977] 1986, 106–7).

The concepts of one's own room and liberation begin to become synonymous for Mira. Her tiny Cambridge apartment, certainly not close to the social status of her husband's spacious house, takes on a comforting and safe ambiance for Mira. As she meets other women at the university and bonds with them, a women's place acquires new significance. The women visit each other's apartments and begin to share each other's lives. They create room for each other even as they expand their own personal space. Amid the rawness that is life, Mira becomes gradually more self-reliant and expands her own room. The growth to maturity is cumulative, and the symbol grows beyond its original meaning to encompass more of life. In the last scene, Mira's room has extended to the out-of-doors—she is at the beach, and she is able to walk along its expanse, unafraid and free.

## Discrepancy in Action between Intention and Outcome

Mira's intent in going to Harvard was to gain a Ph.D. Through the natural unfolding of her time there, she learned more than she expected. She learned her self-worth and gained personal acceptance of the gifts that had been withheld previously from her own view of herself. In the quest for an education, she found herself and was amazed at her value. Here the use of the discrepancy in action between intention and outcome is that of expansion of the goal. Mira is not kept from achieving the education she seeks; rather, she receives much more than she expected. That much more, however, is in keeping with her intention and her nature.

## Moment of Recognition

Mira's liberation takes place through a series of insights or moments of recognition that move her from the nonreflective status of dependent wife and selfless mother to a self-aware woman who finally freely chooses what fulfills her potential as a person. This recognition does not come easily, nor is the newly found consciousness always clear and certain. As Mira grows toward the graced state of liberation as a woman, she must deal with the complexities of her nature and of her milieu.

Mira's sexual nature is one of her most challenging new awarenesses. After a long life of lackluster sex with Norm and then a period of abstinence during which she feels insecure and yearns for a Walter Matthau or an Anthony Perkins to redeem her, Mira recognizes that she can enter into an equalitarian "passionate" love-relationship with Ben. When Ben expresses his wish to have a child with her, Mira is graced with the insight that for her this would be the reemergence of male dominance and complete self-surrender. This is a price too high to pay, given the difficult path to self-individuation that had been thrust upon her when Norm rejected her for a more desirable woman. Saying no to Ben's desire is not a choice against children or a rejection of Ben but a choice toward her own selfhood and liberation.

Having examined French's use of these three literary devices, we can see that the notion of liberation that is depicted is suggestive of a Thomistic understanding of grace.

## *Their Eyes Were Watching God:*
## Augustinian Presentation of Liberation

Presenting an Augustinian understanding of how her protagonist is liberated by grace, Zora Neale Hurston employs the three literary devices in ways very different from French's usage. For Hurston, the need for liberation by the black woman is experienced in the need to reverse reality. Here grace opposes nature in fundamental ways because humankind is seen to be sinful and in need of more dramatic change. In a poignant paragraph, Hurston, through the protagonist Janie's grandmother, Nanny, describes the black woman's condition.

> Honey, de white man is de ruler of everything as fur as Ah been able tuh find out. Maybe it's some place way off in de ocean where de black man is in power, but we don't know nothin' but what we see. So de white man throw down de load and tell de nigger man tuh pick it up. He pick it up because he have to, but he don't tote it. He hand it to his womenfolks. De nigger woman is de mule uh de world so fur as Ah can see. Ah been prayin' fuh it tuh be different wid you. Lawd, Lawd, Lawd. (Hurston [1937] 1978, 29)

Janie's liberation lies in the reversal of her role from society's mule to that of a free woman.

### Symbolization

The horizon and the blossoming pear tree symbolize Janie's vision of marriage, society's assumed destiny for all women.

> From barren brown stems to glistening leaf buds; from the leaf buds to snowy virginity of bloom. It stirred her tremendously. How? Why? . . . She was stretched on her back beneath the pear tree soaking in the alto chant of the visiting bees, the gold of the sun and the panting breath of the breeze when the inaudible voice of it all came to her. She saw a dust-bearing

bee sink into the sanctum of a bloom; the thousand sister-calyxes arch to meet the love embrace and the ecstatic shiver of the tree from root to tiniest branch creaming in every blossom and frothing with delight. So this was marriage! She had been summoned to behold a revelation. (Hurston [1937] 1978, 23–24)

Janie's marriage to Logan Killiks, arranged by Nanny, kills this first dream, though not the feeling rooted in this vision. Early on in the marriage, Janie finds Logan unlovable and physically repugnant. "Janie turned from the door without answering, and stood still in the middle of the floor without knowing it. She turned wrongside out just standing there feeling" (Hurston [1937] 1978, 53). The love that she expected never arrives, though she remembers the vision of the blossoming tree and yearns for its promise. The discrepancy between the symbol and the reality proves so powerful that Janie finally walks out on the marriage, a changed woman.

Janie then takes up with Joe Sparks, who does not represent the blossoming pear tree for her but does speak to her of a far horizon. She links this symbol with her earlier notion of fulfillment and happiness in relationship with a male. But he wants her submission, not her freedom, and slaps her until her ears ring. Years of subsistence with Joe take the fight out of her countenance but not out of her spirit. At Joe's death, she has a third chance to achieve the meaning of the far horizon and of the blossoming tree that had been sown but cut down each time in her relationships. With each deprivation and the suffering that accompanies it, her sense of herself as a woman with needs and expectations grows.

Finally, she takes up with the man who does embody for her the dream so long denied. Her suffering is over. She has come through the contradictions and the humiliation and has been given a partner who loves her and encourages her spirit.

He [Tea Cake] looked like the love thoughts of women. He could be a bee to a blossom—a pear tree blossom in the spring. He seemed to be crushing scent out of the world with his footsteps. Spices hung about him. He was a glance from God. (Hurston [1937] 1978, 161)

## Discrepancy in Action between Intention and Outcome

Janie loves life, the life witnessed in the blossoming pear tree, the life she finally shares with Tea Cake. She has sought it vehemently. Her journey through death-bound relationships to one that finally allows her to live fully, to express herself, and to support life in others has become a willfully chosen mode of acting for growth and fulfillment. But Hurston's powerful story begins and ends with death, Tea Cake's death at Janie's hands.

> So the beginning of this was a woman and she had come back from burying the dead. Not the dead of the sick and the ailing with friends at the pillow and the feet. She had come back from the sodden and the bloated; the sudden dead, their eyes flung wide open in judgment. (Hurston [1937] 1978, 1)

Tea Cake had taken ill, his symptoms gradually worsening until Janie finally calls the doctor. After examining Tea Cake, the doctor gives Janie some pills to give him.

> Give him one of these every hour to keep him quiet, Janie, and stay out of his way when he gets in one of these fits of gagging and choking. . . . I'm pretty sure that was a mad dawg bit yo' husband. It's too late to get hold of de dawg's head. But de symptoms is all there. It's mighty bad dat it's gone on so long. Some shots right after it happened would have fixed him up. . . . Sho is [liable to die]. But the worst thing is he's liable tuh suffer somethin' awful befo' he goes. (Hurston [1937] 1978, 262)

When Janie replies that she loves Tea Cake "fit tuh kill," she does not realize the irony in her words. She intends to do everything and anything to keep Tea Cake alive and to restore his health. But, as Tea Cake worsens, Janie realizes that he is becoming too much to handle, and she grows to fear the mad dog that now inhabits his body. In his delirium, Tea Cake ferociously tries to shoot Janie with a pistol. She desperately takes up a rifle, hoping that when he sees it he will instinctively run. Instead, he fires his gun at her; she fires in self-defense. Tea Cake crumples to the ground, crashing on top of Janie and sinking his teeth into her arm.

> It was the meanest moment in eternity. A minute before she was just a scared human being fighting for its life. Now she was sacrificing self with Tea Cake's head in her lap. She had wanted him to live so much and he was dead. No hour is ever eternity, but it has its right to weep. Janie held his head tightly to her breast and wept. (Hurston [1937] 1978, 273)

What had been Janie's intention is now reversed in a brutal way.

## Moment of Recognition

In seeking the horizon she thought represented her life and her freedom, Janie is brought face to face with death. It is a profoundly personal experience for her. Two instances in the novel, first the death of an earlier lover and then Tea Cake's death—bring her insights that are markedly different. In the first instance, she is saddened and afraid.

> So Janie began to think of Death. Death, that strange being with the huge toes who lived way in the West. The great one who lived in the straight house like a platform without sides to it, and without a roof. He stands in his high house that overlooks the world. Stands watchful and motionless all day with his sword drawn back, waiting for the messenger to bid him come. (Hurston [1937] 1978, 129)

In the event of Tea Cake's death, Janie understands death as a reversal of her earlier fear. Having now seen the horizon, she realizes that the horizon alters death. The horizon sustains her, and she is not afraid. She experiences a moment of vision as the novel closes, and it establishes the peace that begins to abide in her.

> The day of the gun, and the bloody body, and the courthouse came and commenced to sing a sobbing sigh out of every corner in the room; out of each and every chair and thing. Then Tea Cake came prancing around her where she was and the song of the sigh flew out of the window and lit in the top of the pine trees. Tea Cake, with the sun for a shawl. Of course he wasn't dead. He could never be dead until she herself had finished feeling and thinking. The kiss of his memory made pictures of love and light against the wall. Here was peace. She pulled in her horizon like a great fish-net. Pulled it from around the waist of the world and draped it over her shoulder. So much of life in its meshes! She called in her soul to come and see. (Hurston [1937] 1978, 286)

Thus we can see how Hurston's depiction of liberation through her use of the three literary devices suggests an Augustinian notion of the workings of grace.

## *The House of the Spirits:* Jansenistic Presentation of Liberation

In her story of the rise and fall of the Trueba family, Allende uses the three literary devices we are examining to depict a Jansenistic view of how liberating grace operates.

### *Symbolization*

In *The House of the Spirits*, the Trueba family's home serves as a central symbol for the action of liberation that takes place over three generations. The patriarch, Esteban, upon his marriage to Clara, builds a house constructed like the new palaces of North America and Europe, with classical lines but with the comfort of the modern age. He wants it as different from native Chilean architecture as possible, a symbol of his power and ambition.

> [H]e wanted two or three heroic floors, rows of white columns, and a majestic staircase that would make a half-turn on itself and wind up in a hall of white marble, enormous, well-lit windows, and the overall appearance of order and peace, beauty and civilization, that was typical of foreign peoples and would be in tune with his new life. His house would be a reflection of himself, his family, and the prestige he planned to give the surname that his father had stained. (Allende [1982] 1986, 93)

His wife Clara, over whom, like the rest of his family and his workers, he seeks domination, is an elusive clairvoyant whose spirit he can never completely control. Her impact on the family is also represented in her later additions to the house's architecture.

> He [Esteban] could hardly guess that the solemn, cubic, dense, pompous house . . . would end up full of protuberances and incrustations, of twisted staircases that led to empty spaces, of turrets, of small windows that could not be opened, doors hanging midair, crooked hallways, and portholes that linked the living quarters so that people could communicate during the siesta, all of which were Clara's inspiration. Every time a new guest arrived, she would have another room built in another part of the house, and if the spirits told her that there was a hidden treasure of an unburied body in the foundation, she would have a wall knocked down, until the mansion was transformed into an enchanted labyrinth. . . . (Allende [1982] 1986, 93)

With the death of Clara, the house begins to decay. Esteban continues to survive there, a shrunken man, powerless and alone. His sons, Jaime and Nicholas, also live in the house because they have nowhere else to go, but they are indifferent to its condition. Furthermore, they have no interest in the family and no compassion for their father.

Alba, granddaughter to Clara and Esteban through their daughter, Blanca, notices the decay from the first and sees it "advancing slowly but inexorably" (Allende [1982] 1986, 295). But Alba is less concerned with the physical building than she is to recover her grandmother's spirit. This she does, and the elusive spirit of Clara abides with Alba, and Clara's blue silk-covered room becomes the only intact space in the house.

Through the action of liberating grace, Alba is transformed. Like the house itself, she personally undergoes violence and abuse. By the end of the novel, having risked her life to help her lover Miguel in the revolution, having been imprisoned and finally released, raped, battered, and impregnated by one or more unknown assailants, Alba is back in the ruined basement of the Trueba house with the body of her dead grandfather in her arms. His dreams for his house and his family completely destroyed, Alba waits for the return of Miguel and the birth of her daughter. Out of the ruins of the Trueba family and its house, something transformed, completely new and liberating, is being born.

## Discrepancy in Action between Intention and Outcome

Both Esteban and Alba set out on a course of action to achieve their goals. Esteban seeks to establish a patriarchal domain in which he is powerful, wealthy, and respected. He seeks peace and prosperity, even if at the cost of others' lives and goods. For a time he appears to be relatively successful, though violence and treachery often prevail over the steady climb to success he expects.

The turning point on Esteban's path occurs when he beats his daughter Blanca for sleeping with a priest. When he accuses Clara of promoting Blanca's wanton ways, she reminds him of his own libertine life and condemns him for brutalizing the girl. He then strikes his wife. His power is out of control. He immediately realizes this with Clara, but the deed is done. From that time on she falls mute, refusing to speak. Finally she dies, realizing that her mission to change the patron is a failure and her life must come to a close.

Esteban is offered no more grace. His liberation is not accomplished, and he dies a patriarch without a house to rule.

His granddaughter, Blanca's child from her affair with the priest, follows her grandmother's spirit and rises to meet the challenges of grace put in her path. She seeks to foster the cultural revolution as she understands it through her male companion. She is generous and at times very naive. When she volunteers to assist her lover, Miguel, in the cultural revolution that is taking place in Chile, she fails to realize that, as part of the Trueba family, she is identified with the enemy of the people. Furthermore, she is the innocent offspring of Esteban Trueba, who has raped the grandmother of Colonel Garcia, a revolutionary leader. Her transition is from one of privilege to one of victim. By the close of the novel, she is only able to wait for the return of Miguel; the birth of her daughter, the result of many violent rapes; and the emergence of a better time. Alba's tortured body is a sign of the violence of liberation in a revolutionary time. She is no longer able to act but has been acted upon by grace.

## Moment of Recognition

The final moment of recognition belongs to Alba, in the epilogue to the work. She sits at her grandmother's writing table, reflecting on the possible meaning of her own rape by the colonel's grandson. She had earlier thought of revenge on Colonel Garcia, but she begins to question her own hatred.

> I am beginning to suspect that nothing that happens is fortuitous, that it all corresponds to a fate laid down before my birth, and that Esteban Garcia is part of the design. He is a crude, twisted line, but no brush stroke is in vain. The day my grandfather tumbled his grandmother, Pancha Garcia, among the rushes of the riverbank, he added another link to the chain of events that had to complete itself. Afterward the grandson of the woman who was raped repeats the gesture with the granddaughter of the rapist, and perhaps forty years from now my grandson will knock Garcia's grand-daughter down among the rushes, and so on down through the centuries. . . . When I was in the doghouse [being tortured by the revolutionaries she sought to join], I felt as if I were assembling a jigsaw puzzle in which each piece had a specific place. Before I put the puzzle together, it all seemed incomprehensible to me, but I was sure that if I ever managed to complete it, the separate parts would each have meaning and the whole would be harmonious. (Allende [1982] 1986, 431–32)

In response to this insight, Alba believes that her mission in life is to try to reclaim her past through Clara's notebooks, overcome her own terrors, and break this terrible chain of personal and historical events.

Allende's novel is an example of a Jansenistic approach to liberation because liberating grace irresistibly transforms the protagonist's personal life and history.

Though cultural differences among diverse liberation theologies and literatures are often recognized as significant in determining different, even antagonistic approaches to liberation theory and praxis, theological differences are too often neglected. This chapter demonstrates the presence of such theological differences, often subtle and not quickly apparent. By using a hermeneutic analysis of literary devices as they are used in three different stories about women's liberation from oppression, the essay has shown that each of the three has a quite different message to give concerning how liberation is achieved and how it affects the liberated protagonist(s) and their relationships with others. More work needs to be done, of course, but further use of this and similar hermeneutic analyses may be beneficial in furthering an ongoing dialogue among varying approaches to women's liberation.

## References

Allende, Isabel. [1982] 1986. *The House of the Spirits.* Trans. Magda Bogin. New York: Bantam Books.

French, Marilyn. [1977] 1986. *The Women's Room.* New York: Jove Books.

Getz, Lorine M. 1982. *Nature and Grace in Flannery O'Connor's Fiction.* New York: Edwin Mellen Press.

Hurston, Zora Neale. [1937] 1978. *Their Eyes Were Watching God.* Chicago: Univ. of Chicago Press.

# 12

# Theopoetics:
# Longing and Liberation

## Rubem A. Alves

When I was young I believed in the power of clear and distinct ideas. I shared the commonsense belief that misunderstandings live only amidst darkness and mists. I liked Mozart and had problems with Debussy. . . If the ideas are clear, like bright images in a well-polished mirror, and if they are properly knit by logic and evidence, understanding and complicity follow as a matter of fact. Because this is the purpose of language: we want to move out of the sadness of solitude, we want communion. We speak in order to create a community. . .

As I grew older, however, I realized that my expectations could not be fulfilled. Communion is a child of love, and it seems that love shuns too much light. And it came to my mind that there are words which are children of light and belong to the eyes. But the eyes are organs of distance. For one to see, the object must not be too close. One does not kiss with open eyes. . . But there are words which are good to be eaten. The Eucharist, the supreme festival of the Christian tradition, is a meal. The body and the blood of Christ are given, not as objects of thought to be transformed in clear and distinct concepts. They are given to be eaten. Anthropophagy. Communion occurs when one's body is given as food and drink. So I move my words from the classroom, where there is light, to the kitchen, and the alchemic transformations of the raw are prepared for the delight of the body of the other. This, I believe, is the secret of communion: when my body, transformed in words, is given to the other, to be eaten. And as she or he tastes it one says: *It is good.* . . Back to Feuerbach: *Man ist was man isst;* we are what we eat. When the other eats eucharistically a piece of my body, we become "companions," in the original sense of the word: those who eat the same bread.

So I am no longer a professor. I have no lessons to give, no knowledge to communicate. I am a cook. I try to transform my body in words. Indeed, I try to say the words which make up the essence of my being. These statements should not cause any surprise, since they are nothing but a variation of the central motif of the Christian tradition, that *the Word becomes Flesh.* I speak only about myself.

Arrogance? How could someone not feel embarrassed to make such a statement—as if he or she were the center of the world?

I believe, rather, that such a statement implies a great deal of humility. I know nothing about God—I am not a theologian! I know nothing about the world—I am not a scientist. I know only this little space which is my body—and even my body I only see as a dim reflection in a dark mirror.

Confessions.

Not theology. Poetry.

The poet is the person who speaks words which are not to be understood; they are to be eaten. And his stove is his own body lit with the fire of imagination. . .

I speak about this little space, my body, and the universes which live in it, as dreams. "Every artist's strictly illimitable country is himself," says e. e. cummings (Six Non Lectures '69). The poet knows that there is not a universal scientific knowledge to be communicated. His body is the only universal that he knows. As the Brazilian poet Vinicius de Moraes puts it, "nobody can be universal outside one's own backyard garden." If poets speak about stars and mountains, one must know that they have taken them out of their own pockets (Alvaro de Campos). Thomas Mann puts the following words in the mouth of someone, in his *Joseph in Egypt:* "The world hath many centers, one for each created being, and about each one it lieth in its own circle. Thou standest but half a meter from me, yet about thee lieth a universe whose center I am not but thou art." Or as Feuerbach suggested, if flowers could speak they would declare that gods are flowers. The universe of the caterpillars is infinite leaves. . . All symbols we use are symbols about our bodies (Ricoeur).

Maybe this is good Protestant tradition: to know Christ is to know his benefits. *Benefit,* from the Latin *beneficius,* "the good that is done to. . . ."

To know the Wind is to know what it does to my body.

God is the Wind: it comes, it goes, it cannot be put in paper cages or word cages. . . After it goes the only thing which is left is the memory of its touch on my skin. I can only speak about this: reverberations on my body, as it is touched by the Wind; sometimes a chill, sometimes a warm feeling, goose-pimples. . .

Not theology. Poetry. If you like—theo-poetics. . .

"Eat, drink, this is my body, this is my blood. . ."

But my body and blood are a story. No, I am not saying that my body knows stories or tells stories, or likes stories. My body is a story.

To speak about my body is to speak about the stories that make up its soul. The secret of my flesh is a hidden, forgotten text, which is written in it. We are palimpsests. In bygone times, when writing was done on leather, old texts were scraped off and on top of the apparently clean surface, new ones were written, text upon text. . . But the marks of the old stories could never be erased. They remained invisible, inside. . . Today, thanks to science, it is possible to recover them. A good metaphor for what our bodies are. . . stories that are written, scraped off, forgotten, one after another. But even the old ones we believe dead remain alive, and once in a while they puncture the smooth surface of our official stories, as dreams, art, as incomprehensible signs/sighs in the flesh, as madness. . . This is something that psychoanalysis rediscovered. But it was nothing less than an old truth, known to magicians, to poets, and stated in the sacred texts:

The Word became Flesh,
The Poem becomes a Body.
Our flesh is a Word. Our bodies are incarnated poems. . .
No, we do not live by bread only; we must eat words. . .
Poetic is the word which makes love with the body.
When it is spoken, the body trembles,
even though it does not understand it. . .
Magic: when the word has the power to move the flesh.

Emily Dickinson once wrote that when she read a book and it made her whole body so cold no fire could ever warm it, she knew *that* was poetry. If she felt physically as if the top of her head were taken off, she knew that was poetry (474).

The essence of the poetic word lies in its magical power. One does not understand the Wind, and yet the goose pimples appear. . . The poetic word: Wind. . . It performs what it says *ex opere operato*. How? Why? I do not know.

When the body trembles as it hears a word, one may be sure that that word belongs to its soul, it is part of its poem. That tremor is life being resurrected from its slumber.

There is a story—I keep repeating it—and every time I do, the Wind blows again. It was first told by Gabriel Garcia Marques, a *brujo* who knows the alchemy of words and blood: every time he writes, the dead are resurrected. I want to retell it to you, because I have the feeling that it contains the mystery of bodies and souls, the secret of Eros and Thanatos.

It is about a village, a fishermen's village, lost in a nowhere/everywhere, boredom mixed with air, empty words, empty faces, empty bodies, the excitement of love being something no/body remembered. . .

Till one day. . . A boy saw a strange shape floating far away on the sea. And he cried. Everyone came to see. In a place like that anything can be a reason for hope. And there they stayed, on the beach, looking, waiting. Till the sea, slowly, no haste, brought the thing and put it on the sand, to the disappointment of all.

A dead man.

All dead men are alike. And there is one thing only to do: bury them. In that village the custom was that the women prepared the dead for the burial. So, they carried the corpse to a house, women inside, men outside. And the silence was great as they cleaned it from the algae and all the green things of the sea.

But the silence was suddenly broken by a woman.

Had he lived among us he would have had to bend his head every time he entered our houses. He is too tall. . .

The other nodded in approval.
Again the silence was deep until another woman broke it.

I wonder about his voice. Was it like the whisper of the breeze, like the thunder of the waves? Was he that kind of man who knows how to say a word, and because of that word a woman takes a flower and sticks it in her hair?

And they smiled. . .
Silence again. And then, another woman. . .

These hands. . . How big they are! What did they do? Did they play with children? Did they sail through the seas? Did they have tenderness to caress and embrace?

And they laughed and were surprised as they realized that something strange was happening. A movement in their flesh, long believed to be dead, as if magic birds, long forgotten, were flapping their wings again, and joy and desire surfaced on their bodies. They were alive, ready for love again. Their husbands, outside, became jealous of the dead man, because they realized that his silence had a power which they themselves lacked. And they thought about the poems they had never written, the seas they had never seen, the women they had never loved.

The story ends by telling that they finally buried the dead man.

But the village was never the same.
Did you understand the story?
I hope not.
Stories, like poems, are not to be understood.
They are like old trees, to be stood under.
Something which is understood is never repeated.
Like a theorem. . .

Or Agatha Christie's novels: once the riddle is solved, the book is put back on the shelf, never to be read again, forever impotent. But a story which makes the body tremble is like a glass of wine, a Mozart sonata, a poem: to be repeated over and over again. And every time it is repeated the miracle happens anew.

I cannot explain it either.

To explain is to transform mountains and abysses, with their darkness and clouds, in plains under midday sun (from the Latin *ex-planum*). And when the mystery is explained, the only thing which remains is the ex. . .

No. The story does not teach anything. It does not convey any knowledge. It does not communicate information. It cannot be transformed into a doctrine or confession. It cannot be read as a "lesson."

The word which performs the miracle remains unspoken: the dead do not speak. And yet, by the power of this silent mystery—the dead man—the dead-alive were resurrected.

The power to resurrect the dead abides in the silence which lies between the words.

This is what poetry is: words which open up spaces of silence. Not because of silence. But because silence is needed if one is to hear the forgotten poem which is the secret of our body. Everything is said in this marvelous poem by Fernando Pessoa:

Stop your singing!
Stop, because,
as I heard it,
I heard also
another voice
coming from the interstices
of the gentle enchantment
which your singing
brought unto us.

I heard you
and I heard it
at the same time
and different
singing together.
And the melody
which was not there
if I well remember
makes me cry.

Your voice:
was it an enchantment which,
unwillingly,
in this vague moment
woke up
a certain being
to us a stranger
which spoke to us?

I don't know. Don't sing.
Let me hear
the silence
that there is
after your singing.

O! Nothing, nothing!
Only the sorrow
for having heard,
for having wished to hear
beyond the meaning
that a voice has.

Which angel, as you spoke,
without your knowledge
came down to this earth
where the soul wanders
and with his wings
blew the embers
of an unknown home?

Stop your singing!
I wish the silence
to put to sleep
the memory
of the voice I heard,
misunderstood,
which was lost
as I heard it.

*Poesias* 202

Poetry: the spoken poem written on paper to evoke the silent poem written in our flesh.

I read Frost:

The woods are lovely, dark and deep,
But I have promises to keep
and miles to go before I sleep. . . (Frost, 224-25)

I do not understand the magic of its images.

The beautiful, dark and deep woods which make up my soul live dormant in the empty spaces between the trees. And my body is resurrected. . .

Or I read T. S. Eliot:

Our gaze is submarine.
Our eyes look upward
and see the light which fractures through unquiet waters.

I do not understand.

The depth of the sea is not to be understood.

The poem makes me dive into the waters. I feel what it means to be submerged in the mystery of the sea. I am Jonah.

In the poetic experience I live this strange and absurd identity between body and word. I find myself in the magical world.

The medieval theologians were aware of this mystery. In their sacramental theology they spoke about transubstantiation.

Bread and wine, nothing but bread and wine.
A word is spoken.
Poetry. Metaphor.

*This is that:* the formula for a metaphor. The modern scientific mind
is horrified. Nonsense: this cannot be that. . .

This bread is my body.
This wine is my blood.
Nothing seems to change: the "accidents" remain.
And yet everything is different: a new substance.

If we were sensitive to the metaphoric use of language we would
have had visions of this mystery: the identity between word and body.
But we, Protestants, are literalists. We are modern. We have moved
away from the company of poets and magicians, in order to enter the
world of science. And we have missed the point. The revelation of the
secret of the body was dismissed as superstition.

I eat bread, I drink wine.
I don't understand them.

And yet, in spite of my ignorance, they perform the promise they
contain. I am no longer hungry; I become light.

But we do not live by bread and wine only.
We live by the power of the word.

There are words which are not to be thought. They are to be eaten.
I think that the angel, in the book of Revelation, was a poet. And it is
sure that he was not a Protestant, since he was not interested in hermeneutics. . . He gave the little book to the seer and ordered him not
to read, not to understand, not to think about it with clear and distinct
ideas, but to eat it. . .

But we are modern. We have lost the grace of standing under that
which we do not understand. Every mystery must be dissolved by our
doing: we are justified by works. So, we bring in our flashlights to
clarify the darkness of the lovely woods. And after our work is done
we have clear and distinct ideas, but gone is the magic of the darkness.

And we empty the sea, because the light which fractures through
unquiet waters does not meet the standards of clarity and distinctiveness
of the academic world to which we are committed. We are not submarine

beings. We want to be professors. . . We do not abide by the mist-eerie of the poetic silence. We want the light of interpretation.

Interpretation: the text is obscure. Our flashlights are needed.

What did Frost want to say?

What did Eliot want to say?

They wanted but they did not succeed. Poets suffer from a linguistic disturbance. . . This is why the interpreter is needed, to save the poet from his verbal incompetence. Every poem must become scientific discourse. Beauty must become knowledge. . .

Our sanctuaries are symptoms of this vocation: they look more like classrooms, in nothing similar to the Gothic cathedral. One goes inside a cathedral to be touched by the silent voices which abide in its empty spaces. But we go to our sanctuaries to hear the ex-plana-tion of the obscure lessons.

Suppose that a historian lived in that village. A research project would be immediately set up in order to find out precisely what the truth of the dead man was: *Wie es eigentlich gewesen ist*—how it really happened. How did his voice really sound? Did he really travel through unknown seas? Did he really play with children? Did he really love many women?

Suppose that another man lived in the same village. And he was concerned about the ideas of the dead man. He started an investigation in order to find out what his *ipsissma verba* had been, the exact words he had spoken, and the right meanings he had had in mind.

Both were concerned with the scientific, literal meaning of the mystery, because the dreams of the resurrected villagers did not meet the scientific criteria of truth.

After many, many, years of hard work, they returned with their findings in their hands: doctoral dissertations. And they proclaimed the truth. And, as they did it, all the fantasies and poems which had possessed those bodies were dispelled, and the village became again what it had been before the arrival of the dead man. Clear and distinct ideas instead of mists and clouds. Science instead of poetry. An empty sea instead of the submarine gaze. And ex-plained plain instead of the dark woods.

The secret of magic, which is the same of poetry, is this: power does not belong to scientific truth. It belongs to our dreams. "Because dreams is what we are made of" (Brown, 254).

And we could add: dreams are what the universe is made of. God must have dreamed before the creative word was uttered. If God's first word had been only a true statement about what was, our earth would be today still *without form and void, with darkness covering the face of the abyss*. But God was a dreamer. God is the Void where dreams are alive and potent. God dreamed about something that did not exist: a garden. The creative word was a poem, a magical incantation, the purpose of which was to invoke the Absent, which only exists by the power of desire.

Paul Valery, who knew the poetic secret of life, once asked:

"What are we without the help of that which does not exist?"

Or Paul:

God calls the "things that are not in order to bring to nothing things that are."

Poems never tell the scientific truth. They do not describe the existing state of affairs. They say "light," and darkness is gone. They invoke a garden, and deserts are filled with fountains and trees. They pray "children" and the elderly people begin to play. They blow "life" and the dry bones are resurrected.

The Christian community exists around the celebration of an Absence. There have been endless discussions about the mode of Christ's presence in the Eucharist. I want to suggest, however, that this is the wrong issue. The power of the Eucharist is not in a Presence but rather in an Absence. Or, more precisely, in the presence of an Absence.

"Eat and drink till I come back. . . ."

Bread and wine are taken in the joy and pain of this Absence.

Longing: this is the name of the poem which transubstantiates our bodies. And when the body is possessed by Longing its word takes on the form of the naming of an Absence. In classical theological language: prayer. Prayer is the sacred name that we utter before the Void.

I want, thus, to make the following proposition: theology is *not* knowledge of God. How could we know God, if the sacred name is a secret? Theology is the poem that we sing before this mysterious Absence, in order to resurrect the dead. Not theo-logy: theo-poetics.

> And then the Wind carried me out and put me down in a plain
> full of bones.
> And they were very dry.
> Shall these bones live again?
> Prophesy over the dry bones. . . .
> Prophesy to the Wind, prophesy, and say to it:
> O Wind, come from every quarter and breathe into these slain. . . ." (Ezekiel
> 37)

The bones will not be resurrected if they hear the truth about their death. This is why the prophet invokes the Wind. The Wind is Spirit, the dreams once forgotten, that now return. As it happened in the village, by the power of the silence of the dead man. We are resurrected by the power of poetry. . .

Saint Augustine said that a people is "an assemblage of reasonable beings, bound together by a common agreement as to the objects of their love" (Book xix, §24). In our language: a people are those who dream the same dreams.

> As a garden, to be planted, needs a gardener.
> And a gardener is someone who, like God, dreams about gardens.
> So the earth, to be transformed,
> needs many bodies
> which walk and sing following the Cloud which moves ahead.
> Clouds: dreams.
> A politics which is born out of dreaming,
> which is a child of poetry. . . .

I know that this sounds strange—as if I were walking backwards. Have we not learned that we will be saved by truth? Do not we know that politics must be derived from a rigorous, scientific knowledge of "what is"? Is not our task to say with clear and distinct words the truth about the dryness of the dry bones?

> Our world: the fishermen's village,
> The valley of dry bones,
> a barren desert where Thanatos has done her work. . . .
> But Paradise must be recovered.
> And unless the dead become a people, no garden will be planted.

Politics begins not with the administration of the dead but with the resurrection of the dead. I remember the words of Guimaraes Rosa, the greatest of all Brazilian writers:

> The politicians speak all the time about logic, reason, reality. . . . As opposed to them, I believe in men and women, and I wish them a future. I am a writer and think about eternities. The politicians think only about minutes. I think about the resurrection of the dead.

The dead come back to life and become warriors when, inside their bodies, the dream of paradise is remembered. Every battle is a battle for the recovery of the lost garden. Even Marx was aware of that. And he spoke about "breaking the chains" so that we will be able to "cull the living flower." Politics without the dream of a garden inevitably becomes cruel: something of the devil. As Angelus Silesius once put it:

Unless you find Paradise
at your center,
there is not the smallest chance
that you may enter.

A politics out of beauty: it sounds like non-sense. I console myself with Eliot's words:

In a world of fugitives
the person taking the opposite direction
will appear to run away. . . .

And I see the theologian (No! the theo-poet . . .) as someone who, like the dead man of the story, says the poetic word which opens up the infinite space of Longing, in the hope that the dead will become gardeners. So I am trying to develop a theology based on our longings.

Now, what does that have to do with theology of liberation?

The village. The fishermen's village. You can imagine that as the world of the poor. The theologians should be the dead man. The dead woman. Those who are able to provoke dreams. Not to interpret dreams but to provoke dreams. Because we are entities made out of dreams. We are, according to the prologue of John, "the word made flesh," the dream made a body; we are dreams which became bodies. And if people are going to struggle and to fight it is necessary for them to be rocked back to life from their oblivion, and this happens when they are able to dream again. And dreams have always to do with our desires. It is necessary for people to be able to dream again about beautiful things, about utopias, about a new world, because when people are able to dream again then they will be transfigured, they will be resurrected, they will be able to fight. So, although I consider very important the work of analysis, that is not the thing which I am doing right now. I am much more interested in magic and in the lost art of making the word, the dream, the story, incarnated again in the lives of the fishermen, the fisherwomen of that lost village.

## References

Augustine, *The City of God*.

Barthes, Roland. 1975. *The Pleasure of the Text*. Trans. Richard Miller. New York: Hill and Wang.

Brown, Norman O. 1966. *Love's Body*. New York: Vintage Books.

Dickinson, Emily. 1965. Letter #342a. In *The Letters of Emily Dickinson*. Eds. Thomas Johnson and Theodora Ward. Cambridge: The Belknap Press.

Frost, Robert. 1970. *Stopping by the Woods on a Snowy Evening*. In *Poetry of Robert Frost*. Ed. Edward Connery Lathem. New York: Balentine.

Garcia Marques, Gabriel. 1974. El Ahogado mas hermoso del mundo. In *La Incredible y Triste Historia de la Erendira y de su Abela Desalmada*. Barcelona: Barral Editores.

Rosa, João Guimarães, 1983. Literaturae Vida. In *Arte em Revista*. São Paulo CEAC.